DEFIANT RESISTANCE

Defiant Resistance

Shattering the silence on violence against Indigenous women

MARLENE LONGBOTTOM

ABORIGINAL STUDIES PRESS

First published in 2026
by Aboriginal Studies Press

Aboriginal Studies Press (ASP) is the publishing arm of the Australian Institute of Aboriginal and Torres Strait Islander Studies (AIATSIS). ASP acknowledges the spiritual and cultural custodians of the lands upon which ASP operates. ASP acknowledges the Elders and Traditional Owners across all nations and that their sovereignty of their land and water was never ceded. We thank the Elders and knowledge keepers for sharing.

Aboriginal and Torres Strait Islander people are respectfully advised that this publication contains names of deceased people.

GPO Box 553, Canberra, ACT 2601
Phone: (+61 2) 6246 1183
Email: asp@aiatsis.gov.au
Web: aiatsis.gov.au/asp

A catalogue record for this book is available from the National Library of Australia

ISBN 978-1-922752-05-5 (pb)
978-1-922102-87-4 (epub)
978-1-922102-88-1 (epdf)

Cover design: Design by Committee
Text design and typesetting: Tristan Main
Index: Matthew Sidebotham

WARNING

Please be aware that the stories in this book are confronting. They're raw and they speak the truth of the women's realities. For some of you, the subjects I discuss will be shocking. For others, memories of your own personal traumas may resurface. I urge you to care for yourself and understand that you may need to skip parts of the book. Different details are likely to be traumatic for different readers.

Please read these stories without viewing the women and families as victims only. All who have contributed to this book are strong. They're made stronger by what they've lived through and all they've shared — with me and now with you. They are survivors, telling their stories for all to hear. They no longer want to be silenced. Instead, they tell their stories to help others, and as a way to restore their power.

Please do not diminish their stories and voices by ignoring their power. Instead, be strengthened by knowing that you may be able to help someone by sharing these stories or the knowledge you learn from reading them.

Again, please take care of yourself as you read. You may need to put the book down for a time. You may need to reach out to loved ones or find help through support systems or emergency services. Please remember that you are not alone. There are people who can and will help you. Please be safe.

Aboriginal and Torres Strait Islander people are respectfully advised that this book contains the names of women who have died.

13YARN (24/7) — call 13 92 76 to connect with an Aboriginal or Torres Strait Islander Crisis Supporter.

1800RESPECT (24/7) — call 1800 737 732 or text 0458 737 732 for free and confidential counselling, information and referral service for anyone in Australia impacted by domestic and family violence.

If you're in immediate danger, please call 000.

CONTENTS

ACKNOWLEDGEMENTS

I acknowledge the communities and the First Nations peoples whose lands, knowledges, and stories ground this work. I pay my respects to Elders past and present, and to the communities whose strength, wisdom and lived experiences have guided the reflections in this book.

To the women who have contributed to this book: without your stories, this work would never have been possible. There is life after violence, and I hope I have carried your stories with the respect, love and care they deserve. To the families of Allira, Baby Jai, Crystal and Florrie, thank you for sharing your loved ones with me. I hold that trust with the greatest honour and deepest responsibility. To everyone I have spoken with in writing of this book, and to those I have met along the journey who shared their stories with me personally—thank you for trusting me to hold and honour your truths.

My heartfelt thanks go to Katungul Aboriginal Corporation Community & Medical Services, Illawarra Aboriginal Medical Service, Yerin Aboriginal Health Service, Waminda South Coast Women's Health and Wellbeing Aboriginal Corporation and the Queensland Indigenous Family Violence Legal Service. Your work in the community, particularly your unwavering commitment to the wellbeing and self-determination of Aboriginal and Torres Strait Islander women, families and communities, has strengthened the purpose behind every page.

To my cousins Kirsty and Bud, our Nan would be so proud of all of us.

To my mum, thank you for always being in my corner and reminding me of who I am and the love of Nan and Farthy.

To my son Jarrah, nieces Jean and Mary, nephews Eddie and Keron, grandchildren, and my partner, Frank—without your love and support, for being my safe space, the constant check-ins, the gentle push to keep going, the cooked meals and the shared exhaustion—this book would not have been possible. Thank you for holding me up in every way.

To Kathie Clapham, Bronwyn Fredericks and John Maynard, thank you for believing in me and supporting my academic endeavours from the very beginning of my career. To Aunty Mandy and Uncle Ray Kelly, thank you for being the cultural mentors and the ear that I needed. To my IERC family, Sana Nakata and Felicia Watkin Lui, thank you for keeping me grounded and on track, and for helping me articulate the often intangible complexities that our communities experience. My sincere thanks to Martin Nakata, whose mentoring and guidance helped me see what I could not yet see, and who continues to challenge me to deepen my knowledge. And to Aileen Moreton-Robinson, thank you for your support, your leadership, and for illuminating a gap in the body of knowledge that inspired this work.

Lastly, thank you to the ancestors, who have guided and held me along this journey called life.

This book is dedicated to Nan, whose love carried me in my darkest of times, and who gave me her blessing and pushed me to get an education when she said, 'Education is the way of the white man, go get educated Marl.'

INTRODUCTION: DEFYING VIOLENCE

How did I get here? How did I come to write a book about violence and decide to focus on this area of research, given my lived experience? It's kind of a long story — and it's one I touch on throughout this book. I think this is something I was chosen to do. I have a passion for ensuring Indigenous women are respected and afforded the love and care they deserve. Those who understand the way ancestors operate know that when you've been chosen, things just fall into place. My journey through life has led me to the work I do today. I firmly believe the ancestors have chosen me to share the stories told in this book, including my own story. I am a Yuin woman, a mother, grandmother, sister, cousin and aunty. I am also an Indigenous researcher.

I have also had my share of troubles throughout my life. When I was fifteen, I attempted suicide after being raped. I woke up from the overdose, and I believe I woke for a reason. Helping others to share their stories is my purpose. Thankfully, I lived to tell my story, which could have ended that night. But the ancestors had another plan for me.

This book brings together my story and the stories of other Indigenous women who have experienced violence. This is not an easy topic to address and not an area of research just anyone can do. How I got here, though, is a combination of personal and professional purposes. Firstly, being open to hearing the advice of mentors, and secondly, wanting to make a personal contribution to ensuring the safety in our communities as Indigenous women. The more formal process of conducting research about violence was something that drew me in. A mentor and leading Indigenous scholar, Distinguished Professor Aileen Moreton-Robinson, suggested that I look at violence in our communities and advised me about a gap in the body of knowledge regarding what violence is and how it has changed throughout time. Also, how we as Indigenous peoples have bought into such understandings. I knew I wanted my research to have significance and that I wanted to help our communities, that I wanted to help others.

Early in my research career, I identified the type of research I didn't want to do. I didn't want to conduct pathologising research that focuses on the deficit and dysfunction in our communities — the type that is often reported and written about in the media. As a survivor of violence, I felt I needed to share my story and help others who have experienced violence. I started my research career working in Aboriginal community-controlled services and soon realised that my experiences and the experiences of other survivors needed to be heard.

I view myself as a survivor, not a victim. Like all the women and families in this book, I am strong and powerful — and that strength is the key to my work. My passion and drive come from hearing traumatic stories and wanting to ensure they are shared in a way that honours women and children with respect and dignity.

A few years after I started this research, while doing my PhD, I remember being immersed in data for what I think of as the 'trauma chapter'. I was deeply engaged with stories of trauma and analysing women's experiences of violence. As I completed each interview, the trauma stories were transcribed into a document for me to read, reread and analyse. At this stage, I had yet to interview the families whose loved ones had been killed. As you will read in the coming pages, the impact of this work is heavy. Eventually, the trauma stories merged — not only did I have my own story and nightmares of the violence I experienced, but I also now had the stories I'd heard. Going to sleep at night was scary, and after reading the transcripts of the women's stories, I began to experience more nightmares. Sometimes I even feared sleeping, wondering when the next nightmare would come and whose story it would be. Would my nightmare be about my personal trauma or something connected to the women's stories? Or would it blur into one?

Another unanticipated consequence of this research was my crying — deep, ugly-face crying. During this period, I would stop and start with my writing. I got angry. I remember punching the keyboard, tears streaming down my face. These moments were hard, but at the same time, pivotal. I came to realise that if I stopped, the stories would stop with me. I realised my responsibility to the women who had shared their stories. I needed to make sure their stories were heard. Thus, I continued through the trauma chapter and now, ten years later, I am researching other aspects of violence.

I remember praying to my ancestors while I was writing the trauma chapter. One day, in tears, I sat on the edge of my bed and asked, 'Why do I have to do this work?' The epiphany came in that moment: I had been chosen. In my prayer, I said to the ancestors, 'Okay, so you've chosen me. Guide my footsteps and I will follow your path wherever you take me.' From that moment, I accepted my fate and the enormous responsibility that comes with this work. I must honour the stories I was privileged to hear. But doing this work was like a seesaw at times — or perhaps like being on a merry-go-round of emotions. It was hard to not become emotional and feel empathy with the women who shared their stories. At the same time, I was inspired by the women, their achievements, their strength, their outlook on life and their success in life after violence. They had all overcome obstacles placed in front of them by the perpetrators of violence and by the services and systems that failed them (and continue to fail Indigenous women today).

I am now able to share these stories with you and the world. Providing a platform for the stories, alongside careful theoretical analysis, allows women and families to share their experiences in a judgement-free environment and fosters a narrative that does not polarise or pathologise their lives. Through this book, I seek to restore their power while simultaneously honouring my responsibility to them. All the women and families I spoke with have entrusted me with their stories — to hold them and share them. This is a huge responsibility that I do not take lightly.

STORIES AND YARNING – A TOOL FOR HEALING

In my research, I have come to learn that stories can be productive. Many of the women and families I have spoken with explained that sharing their stories was part of their healing journey. I also draw from the work of Australian and international Indigenous scholars whose work centres the voices of Indigenous people. I draw inspiration from the words of Mohawk scholar Professor Audra Simpson (2016), who focuses on Indigenous people's perspectives and speaks about the right of refusal. By drawing on the work of Simpson and others, I am able to ask deeper questions relating to politics, place and who is afforded privilege. By drawing on such work, I want to define who I am and support the women and families who have shared their stories with me. I want to ensure that their experiences of talking with me provide an opportunity for *them* (us) to tell *their* (our) stories *their* (our) way. We refuse to be defined by our experiences. We refuse to be silenced.

Restoring power to Indigenous women motivates my work. The women who shared their stories with me are amazing and beautiful. They are my sisters and aunties. They are powerful and strong. In our discussions they drew on humour — yarning and laughing helped us to face the realities of trauma. Our yarns left me in awe, feeling privileged to have shared these moments. I hope that as you read, you will feel the same. I hope you're reminded of the women in your life who have shared their stories.

Speaking up and out is something that Indigenous women do daily. We've done it for thousands of years. Much of my work is driven by my passion for Indigenous women's labour and what we do for our families and communities. Through my work, I want to ensure women have an opportunity to speak back to those who cause them harm — to the system, the perpetrators and those who stand alongside the perpetrators. By telling their stories, the women in this book contribute their experiences to assist others.

Being involved in this type of project places multiple burdens on those who have experienced violence, and requires a trauma-informed, culturally sensitive, responsive approach. To culturally ground this work, I used yarning to create a safe and supportive environment (Bessarab and Ng'andu 2010; Fredericks 2008). Yarning is a research method, but it's also a culturally grounded way of approaching the topic with each contributor and provides a process for discussing confronting matters. From a cultural perspective, yarning is a way of communicating between two or more people. It can be a formal or informal exchange of information or the sharing of stories. Many people use the term colloquially to describe a conversation, but for Indigenous people across the country a yarn can mean different things, depending on context.

In the yarning interviews, I asked some specific questions, but other topics simply arose. As we moved through the yarns, these issues were elaborated and explored further. Our yarns covered topics like the women feeling judged in connection to their Indigeneity, the negative impacts of some service providers, and racism and discrimination. We spoke about what made it easier to report violence and the services that supported them. We focused on how the women navigated these experiences, and their comments became an important part of understanding their stories.

Each yarn I conducted was held individually. This took time but was vital — a group setting could not have produced the depth and detail I needed and would not have offered the necessary confidentiality.

Individual yarns provided a safe space where I could hear each story and give each woman an opportunity to share her story in the way she wanted.

My responsibility in sharing these stories includes safety and legal considerations. Many of the women experienced some form of police, judicial or family law matter. I held the yarns in safe places, where confidentiality could be kept, and after the yarns I checked in with the women to ensure they had not been impacted negatively. When I reached out to follow up after the interview, we had a general yarn about what they had going on and whether they needed further support. I've maintained a relationship with some of the women who participated, while others just wanted to share their story and put that part of their life to rest. Overall, the feedback I received was that taking part in the yarns was a positive experience for their healing journey. I hope that each woman feels a sense of accomplishment and that they all felt heard and not judged. With each participant, I share an understanding that I hold with the greatest respect. If I happen to see them in my travels, we yarn like old friends.

Ensuring safety and confidentiality

As a researcher, I have ethical responsibilities to the women and families who shared their stories. Women have been violently murdered. I do not want to compromise the lives of their families, so my approach to this work is one of safety. I include direct quotes from the women to ensure their voices are amplified and heard, and to provide their voices as a possible intervention for other survivors who read this work. The women openly shared their experiences with me, and I was determined to honour their voices and maintain the richness and depth of their experiences. Quite simply, these women have called for their voices to be heard. They expect to be heard.

I am mindful that certain aspects of the women's stories could potentially identify them. Community members reading this book may know some of the stories and may be able to connect this book to them.

I have not altered any stories, but I have removed names, places and information that could be linked to a specific community or story. For the safety of the women and their families, I have deidentified the data and taken extreme care to maintain confidentiality. For these same safety reasons, specific details, such as demographics, organisations and locations, are not discussed. What can be shared is that all the women were Indigenous and aged between 30 and 58 at the time of interviews. They were mothers, with a few being grandmothers. The women experienced violence across the continuum, mostly as young women or young mothers (not at the ages they were when I interviewed them). At the time of the interviews, they had left their violent relationships, with the most recent experience of violence taking place at least three years before the interview.

I have assigned pseudonyms to most of the women, using names that are grounded in beauty, strength and power, and that come from Indigenous communities around the world. But some women want to be known and we — me and my cousin Kirsty, our cousin Bud, and Melissa, Tom, Nardia and Lachlan — have chosen to share our names. In Chapter 8 I include the stories of two Aboriginal women and one Torres Strait Islander woman who passed away as a result of violence. I use the real names of the women and their families, as the families wished to honour their loved ones. Allira Green — along with her unborn child, Baby Jai — Crystal Ratcliffe and Florrie Reuben were women whose families loved them dearly. Their stories are told in the ways their families want them told.

TELLING THEIR (OUR) STORIES

At times, the women said they were unsure of where or how to tell their stories. Through this work, they were able to share their perspectives in the ways they wanted. Previously, their stories had been told in ways that were directed by others, such as in police reports. Yarning gave the women time to reflect on their strengths and the journeys they had overcome.

> I've always wanted to help people through the situation I went through, but I've never really got to the point where I've ... I've just told people what's happened to me but never in a formal sort of context. (**Jaylah**)

> I didn't know how to share my story, I didn't know who to tell, I didn't know how to communicate, you know what I mean? I didn't know who I could turn to and then when I spoke about my story, things started coming together when I spoke about, when I wasn't afraid to talk about it, things started happening for me for the better. (**Lani**)

Part of the difficulty of sharing stories relates to the long history of Indigenous women being perceived as explicitly sexualised and promiscuous. There is also a common idea linking these stories to shame. Holding onto their stories and not speaking of specific events is a way of protecting those close to them from the vicarious or secondary trauma of hearing about what happened. So, while it was difficult to share their stories publicly, in some cases the women censored their experiences to protect others, including their families and loved ones.

> What made it difficult is like, would they believe you? Why would I want to tell my mum and dad and friends I was sleeping under the bed? Alright, I'm being sexually forced to submit and whatever. Like, you don't tell that sort of stuff to the people that really love and care for you and that are the closest to you. (**Anika**)

> It's kind of one of those stories that I like to keep to myself. I just tell people I've been through shit, I've had my experiences of different types of trauma throughout my life as a child and maybe there will be one day where I disclose it in a public forum but, right now, this is the first kind of public way in which I've shared my story to help other women. But maybe one day I'll tell that story. (**Jaylah**)

> I'm still on my healing journey and I never offered out my story, I never have shared my real story with anyone else before so I hadn't had an opportunity to share it cos I hadn't felt heard. (**Keira**)

When we spoke, the women were in a healthy space mentally and emotionally — they were well along their healing journey and able to speak about their experiences. This was a vital part of the process as I didn't want to risk retraumatising the women. For me personally, I've become tired of reliving these experiences. I was diagnosed with complex post-traumatic stress disorder and anxiety. So, when it comes to sharing my lived experience, I tend to just let people know I have experienced violence and stop at that. My experiences aren't for everyone, and I'm conscious of how my story can impact others. Along with what comes personally for me when I share.

My story is but one in this book. It doesn't take precedence over any other story. My story is part of a collective. Our communities have become closed off to talking about violence, and in some communities, it is often taboo to speak about it. Stories being kept in silence or unspoken holds the survivor hostage. It robs them of the ability to heal and be heard. My story of violence includes police, courts and people who used violence. At different stages I've had some justice and in other cases none. But one thing that is certain is that my story is mine. This book shares the stories of many other Indigenous women and families as well.

LET'S GET THIS STRAIGHT

As you will see, I am not one to be silent about injustice, particularly violence. I have a straightforward manner in discussing the issues that confront our communities daily. I make no apologies for my stance. When I hear that yet another Indigenous woman is fighting for her life in hospital or has been killed, I feel for the children left behind and the families who are thrust into the media spotlight or left engaging with systems that often let them down. In many ways, I dislike researching the topic of violence. But the issue has become so widespread that we need to unpack why and how, so we can begin to examine what to do to make sure Indigenous women are respected and can live safely.

Violence in Indigenous communities is multilayered and complex. Not in the sense that it is hard or difficult to talk about — in fact, it's quite easy to talk about — but because there is no simple solution. The violence experienced by Indigenous women is endemic (AIHW 2026). It occurs in a discursive or circular manner. It is interconnected like a web, with connections at multiple levels — individual, relationship, familial, community, societal, systemic and structural. Often, this web of interconnectedness is overlooked while society focuses entirely on a single response — like a crisis response or prevention or some other intervention that tackles one issue without understanding the wider complex environment. What is missing in the national discourse about violence in Indigenous communities are more firsthand accounts from survivors themselves where large numbers of voices are brought together in one place and centred. There are four points I wish to make clear from the start.

Indigenous women are not complicit, we are silenced

We — Indigenous women — do not accept nor tolerate violence. Of any sort. It is a common narrative that Aboriginal and Torres Strait Islander communities tolerate violence — and even accept it as a normal part of life. While there are broad community issues with violence, this narrative of tolerance and acceptance is deeper, more nuanced and rooted in history. It's based on rumours asserting that women are complicit. This couldn't be further from the truth. Countless Indigenous women have advocated against violence, some of whom are self-identified survivors. Claims of women's complicity are harmful and form a dominant and influential discourse. More importantly, they silence Indigenous women. People who experience violence are usually encouraged to not speak about it because of the shame it brings to their families or communities. However, speaking about violence and its consequences is vital to ensuring our communities become places of safety.

Sharing the stories of survivors comes with responsibility. While there is a risk of retraumatisation, sharing stories through conversations is a way of exploring answers to address the issue. Silencing is often imposed by perpetrators, by sections of the community, or by structural and systemic issues in the broader community (Longbottom et al. 2016). In a supportive, trauma-informed and safe environment, survivors can openly share their stories in depth. In this book, several women talk about their experiences of sharing their stories as part of their healing journey. For some, talking to me was the first time they had spoken openly outside their support networks about the violence they encountered. Indigenous women are ready to speak. When they do speak, it is from a position of strength, power and love.

Language has power

We need to understand the power and impact of language, and how it binds us as individuals or communities. Sometimes, matters of vulnerability and social issues surface that do not present Indigenous people and communities in the most admirable light. Quite naturally, we do not want to speak ill of or think badly of our loved ones, families, friends or broader community. If language is misused, it can hold people hostage to certain descriptions or ways of understanding. For example, I do not call myself a victim. I describe myself as a person with lived experience or a survivor. If I allow language to hold me to the position of victim, I could create a narrative of victimhood, in which I should be pitied and I am weak. If I become a victim, I do not control the narrative about myself. From this perspective, my voice and story are no longer present, and I become silenced into the framing of victimhood that others have created for me.

Language binds people to certain ideas — like when a woman is in a relationship that is difficult to leave. The common misconception is that she 'chooses' to be in unsafe situations. Here, ignorance becomes the problem. It creates a form of imposed silence that traps Indigenous women and makes them hostage to the narratives created about them. These narratives have produced labels such as the 'battered woman syndrome'. They are often negative and remove agency and strength from the people who experience violence. Thus, it is vital to ensure that Indigenous women can speak freely, using language they know, to share their stories authentically in spaces that are supportive and safe.

My responsibility is to amplify women's voices

As I said earlier, this work comes with responsibility — something I do not take lightly. My role in sharing these stories is not one of ownership. Nor is it my intention to impose my voice over the voices of the women. Rather, I amplify their voices, providing them with a safe space to share their lived realities and speaking as both individuals and as a collective. I aim to ensure their multiple identities — for example, being both Indigenous and women — are discussed in their stories. This approach highlights the duality of many women as being hypervisible in some circumstances yet invisible in others (particularly in their contact with systems). The duality becomes more prominent when they seek assistance from non-Indigenous services.

I firmly recognise the agency of Indigenous women and their families, and their fundamental right to shape their own narratives. I aim to create pathways for change that will benefit future generations of Indigenous women, their children and their families. The women and families I spoke to expressed a heartfelt hope that, by sharing the stories of their loved ones, they can save lives and foster a deeper understanding of the challenges they faced.

The stories in this book are a profound challenge to society, urging us all to recognise Indigenous women and families who have survived violence and homicide as proactive and unwavering individuals who are active agents in their own lives. By centring their voices and experiences, this work emphasises the importance of self-determination and highlights how they have intentionally constructed their narratives. This focus is crucial, as it lays the groundwork for meaningful interventions that genuinely support Indigenous women and children. By showcasing their strength and agency, this book advocates for approaches that acknowledge and empower Indigenous communities and ensure future support systems are responsive and culturally nuanced.

Women who speak up need to be heard

Speaking about violence is met with varied responses in communities. Some people are supportive and hold space for survivors. Others want silence. Regardless of the various views and beliefs, violence is insidious. When provided the space to speak, survivors share insights into what is required to address the issues and become a source of inspiration for others who may have similar experiences.

> I think for Indigenous women's voices to be heard more, we need more Indigenous women working in this sort of service ... to get the word out there and to help as many people as we can and then all those success stories coming through, maybe telling their story and inspiring some more Indigenous women to let them know and keep branching out. (**Jemila**)

Often, women with shared experiences become part of a support system for others. These roles in community are pivotal. Shared experiences often provide a level of understanding between survivors and service personnel, where trusting relationships can be developed, and women feel as though they can speak without the added pressure or fear of being judged.

> I feel very blessed and very privileged to be in the space that I am. That I can help women make a difference, particularly in my community. It took me a couple of years to work out what my purpose was supposed to be and now that I've found my purpose, I realise that my struggles that I've been through have prepared me for what I'm doing now. (**Jaylah**)

AS YOU READ

As you read this book, you will see that there is no 'typical' form of violence. Each woman's story of violence is different, and those who look for 'typical' violence minimise the experiences of survivors. Lani experienced violence as an adult in an intimate relationship with her children's father but had no violence in her home as a child. Anika experienced violence from the very beginning of her relationship. Florrie Reuben, Crystal Ratcliffe, Allira Green and Baby Jai were murdered. These stories demonstrate a continuum of violence in the lives of Indigenous women in Australia. There is no one specific type, nor is there a distinctive frequency. It happens when it happens.

We, as a community, need to be ready to provide support when violence does occur. We need to call out those who use violence. Violence should not be tolerated. Once identified, something needs to be done about it. My message to you, the reader, is this: do not minimise any survivor's story. Understand that these experiences are horrific and should be treated with the utmost respect.

As part of the research process, a researcher is required to immerse themselves in the data. For me, this meant immersing myself in the stories of the women and their families. It resulted in nightmares and sleepless nights, which my mentors told me were a normal part of the process. I kept asking myself, 'How normal is normal?' and, 'What even is normal?' The violence I heard about was not normal. And it was not okay that the women and families had experienced it. Nor was it okay that the service system let them down and failed to protect women and families.

The stories in this book are raw and provide a firsthand account of Indigenous women's experiences in their relationships and support networks. I ask that you read, from this point forward, with caution, as the stories may trigger your own trauma. Most importantly, read knowing that the women and families in this book are survivors.

I've spent a lot of time thinking about how best to share the stories, and have talked with the women, families, colleagues, my own family and friends. This has been to ensure I stay true to what was shared with me, while also understanding how I should honour each woman's story. I aim to maintain their authentic voices while revealing the macro environment and the histories and policies Indigenous women have experienced. Documenting the past allows the present to be understood in context.

As you read, I ask you, again, to be aware that the stories in this book are confronting. While the women and their families tell their stories throughout this book, I present most of the stories in Part B. Feel free to skip straight to these personal experiences if you like — or to skip them entirely if you feel unready or unable to read them.

This book is for the women who have shared their stories and for the women who are no longer with us — Florrie, Crystal and Allira and Baby Jai — and for their families.

ANGER — A USEFUL EMOTION

Anger can serve as a powerful catalyst for change. However, misdirected anger or emotional dysregulation can lead to harmful consequences — sometimes even fatal ones. Throughout my individual experiences and my work, I have harnessed anger in various ways. I see this book as a productive way of channelling my anger into meaningful work. However, at moments I allowed my anger to manifest in dysregulated ways, with results that are considered violent.

Anger can drive us to address critical issues. Without anger, people may not be compelled to confront the violence experienced by Indigenous women and children. I believe it's appropriate to allow anger to underscore the urgency of the situation facing Indigenous women. By channelling this anger into productive action, we can work towards fostering awareness and influencing change for those who experience violence and oppression.

A MESSAGE FROM JAYLAH

> If there's one message I want to share, it's about self-love, loving yourself and understanding what a healthy and respectful relationship is. If your needs aren't getting met ... As much as you love that person and as much as you want to see the good parts of them, there's also the not-so-good parts of them. You need to weigh up whether you can deal with that. Violence of any sort ... Whether it's financial, emotional, physical, sexual, all that sort of stuff, that's not a healthy relationship. I want to remind our women about the power that they hold. That they are powerful. They're strong, they're loved, and most of all, that they're valued. (**Jaylah**)

PART A

An Imposed Culture of Violence

CHAPTER 1

THE INFRASTRUCTURE OF VIOLENCE

> I think from colonisation, from white men, it was abusive ... white men taking black women and abusing them, mentally, physically and sexually, and then that was portrayed and passed on to be acceptable when it wasn't accepted ... I think it's contributed to some of the dirtiest acts that have happened to us ... like how the white man would rape the women ... the young men were raped and they're not going to talk about that. (**Lani**)

Since invasion, Aboriginal and Torres Strait Islander women have lived within — and adapted to — a violent culture imposed upon them, including the embedding of Western patriarchal systems. Women like Lani describe violence in ways that go beyond physical assault and include the cultural normalising of abuse and the long afterlife of that violence across generations. These stories, and those shared by the women and families in this book, set a scene that separates the violence experienced by Indigenous women from that experienced by others in this nation.

While I acknowledge that non-Indigenous women — and both Indigenous and non-Indigenous men — also experience violence, my focus here is specifically on Indigenous women. This is because the ways systems respond to Indigenous women are different, shaped by racialised assumptions, gaps in support and long-standing institutional failures.

By centring Indigenous women's stories, I honour the lives, experiences and knowledges of those who have contributed to this book. Prioritising their stories is essential. Their voices reveal forms of harm and systemic neglect that non-Indigenous women do not experience in the same way. I make no apologies for taking this stance. If you are looking for a book that softens what Indigenous women have lived through, or treats violence as something too uncomfortable to name, then this is not that book. This book speaks the truth, plainly, because silence has never kept Indigenous women safe.

The stories shared with me make it clear that Indigenous women are navigating multiple forms of violence that call for constant survival work — thinking ahead, planning, making hard decisions and acting in ways that keep themselves and their families as safe as possible. Some people might be quick to call the women in this book 'resilient'. But that word can flatten their experiences. It risks placing the burden back onto the woman, instead of recognising the violence they were forced to negotiate and the limited choices available to them. In some situations — as I discuss later — the safest option for a woman was to stay in a violent relationship until a moment arose when leaving could be done more safely.

What I want to show in this book is that responding to violence against Indigenous women is far from simple. It's not that violence can't be discussed — it must — but singular, one-off programs and short-term interventions will not address the issue. Responses that lean primarily on policing and legal reforms also fail to deal with the realities Indigenous women face when systems misread violence, misidentify victims and respond to violence through incident-based thinking over patterns of coercive control (Nancarrow 2020; Cripps 2022). Indigenous women are still being killed. National homicide monitoring data show Aboriginal and Torres Strait Islander women experience homicide victimisation rates up to seven times the national average and are most likely killed by someone they know — often an intimate partner (Bricknell and Miles 2024).

Any meaningful response has to take all of this into account, because dealing with violence in isolation from these realities will never address what Indigenous women are living through.

Understanding how Indigenous women are socially constructed and perceived is important. That is because these ideas influence how Indigenous women are treated, how their experiences are interpreted and whether they are offered support. Many dominant constructions have not come from Indigenous women themselves. Instead, they have been created, repeated and reinforced through external narratives (Moreton-Robinson 2000). Some of these constructions have been adopted and adapted by Indigenous women and communities over time. These ideas set expectations about how Indigenous women are supposed to behave, how they should speak, how they should react to harm and how they (we) carry themselves in public. These expectations shape who is believed, who is judged and who is dismissed.

When it comes to violence, these perceptions matter deeply. They influence whether Indigenous women are viewed as 'credible', whether they are treated as worthy of protection and whether systems respond at all. They also shape the narrow idea of the 'ideal' victim — a standard few Indigenous women are afforded (Christie 1986). When a survivor falls outside these accepted parameters, systems often struggle to recognise her experiences and support becomes harder to access. This is not accidental; it is the outcome of long-standing narratives created by others about Indigenous women, but never defined by Indigenous women themselves (Moreton-Robinson 2000).

As Indigenous Australian scholars have written, Western constructions — sometimes described as inscriptions — have shaped the way Indigenous people are known and interpreted within dominant institutions (Nakata 2007). These inscriptions are often imposed and built on cultural misconceptions, including misconceptions about Indigenous women's roles within their own societies and the ways those roles are measured against white womanhood (Moreton-Robinson 2000; Nakata 2007). Over time, these narratives have overridden Indigenous women's authority to define who they are, how they wish to be identified and how they behave and participate in society (Moreton-Robinson 2000). I make clear throughout this book that Indigenous women have their (our) own agency: we can articulate our own experiences and we can speak for ourselves.

From an Indigenous perspective, Indigenous women are often understood to be the backbone of community. Across communities, people speak openly about women's strength and those statements are common enough to be well accepted. For many Indigenous women, this is not new information. Moreton-Robinson (2000) wrote about Indigenous women's standpoint and the ways white feminist frameworks position Indigenous women, showing how Indigenous women speak back and reclaim authority over their own representation, in her critical text *Talkin up to the white woman* more than twenty years ago.

Likewise, Torres Strait Islander scholar Martin Nakata identifies how Western inscriptions have framed Torres Strait Islander people in ways that do not represent Islanders' own understandings of themselves. Nakata writes about the complexity of Torres Strait Islander spaces, places, times and relations — including how Torres Strait Islanders have been known, defined and understood by non-Indigenous people, often through observation from within the dominant worldview rather than through Islander knowledge systems (Nakata 2007).

The imposed inscription across the frontier and colonial period included narratives that cast Indigenous people as violent and barbaric (Nakata 2007). At the same time, colonial collecting practices involved the taking of ancestral remains and cultural material, including grave disturbances and the removal of objects without consent. These acts were not isolated or benign; as Lui-Chivizhe's work on nineteenth-century Torres Strait collections shows, the removal of cultural belongings and ancestral remains was embedded in broader colonial logic that treated Indigenous cultural items as materials to be extracted (Lui-Chivizhe 2022). This raises the questions that must be asked: Who was labelled violent? Who did the taking? And who benefited from the stories that were told?

How have these inscriptions become so ingrained in modern understandings of Indigenous people in Australia? I assert that these ideas develop from the work of those who first recorded their observation of Indigenous Australians. These writers were outsiders to Indigenous societies and interpreted what they saw through their own cultural lens and framing. Indigenous people were written about, spoken for, described and analysed. Cultural processes and protocols were misunderstood and misconstrued by Western observers (Nakata 2007; Maynard 2007). Yet their observations have been accepted, to varying degrees, as truth. Indigenous scholars continue to speak back to these inscriptions and challenge their authority (Moreton-Robinson 2000; Nakata 2007).

French philosopher Michel Foucault argues that societies operate through 'regimes of truth' — systems that decide what counts as true and who has the authority to declare it (Foucault 1980). In his account, each society privileges certain discourses as truths, establishes mechanisms for distinguishing true from false statements, applies sanctions, elevates certain techniques for producing truth and authorises particular speakers as truth-tellers (Foucault 1980). Using Foucault's framing, it becomes possible to analyse how Western-Anglo-Celtic dominance has shaped Australia's social, cultural and political landscape and, in doing so, has contributed to producing what gets treated as the national 'norm'. That norm becomes the benchmark against which others are measured and compared, and it creates the conditions for Indigenous knowledge to be treated as secondary, alternative or 'other' — even when those knowledges are foundational.

Who 'owns' or 'writes' the truth resonates deeply across society. It is visible in the writing of Australian history and the way knowledge about Aboriginal and Torres Strait Islander peoples and cultures has become known through Western lenses. Historical representation has repeatedly privileged non-Indigenous interpretations over Indigenous accounts, producing reductive and inaccurate portrayals that do not capture cultural depth and lived experience (Maynard 2007; Nakata 2007). In more recent years, Indigenous people have increasingly reclaimed and told stories from Indigenous standpoints. This was one of the underlying needs for a book such as this. This shift matters, not as an abstract academic exercise, but because narrative control has real consequences, including for the safety of women and children.

This leads to the intersection between violence and representations of Indigenous women. With violence, as with other issues, dominant understandings are often rooted in Western-Anglo-Celtic frameworks. As a result, Indigenous women have been positioned within contradictory stereotypes: cast as subordinate and dependent, while simultaneously constructed as non-ideal victims. These constructions shape how institutions and agents within respond to violence and how they decide whose harm 'counts'.

Accepted narratives dictate how a 'true' victim of crime should behave, appear and present their case. Research on domestic and family violence system responses shows that institutional processes can misread women's resistance and survival strategies, including by misidentifying victim-survivors as perpetrators — a problem that disproportionately affects Aboriginal and Torres Strait Islander women (Nancarrow 2020). This is also demonstrated in the stories that follow in this book.

These conflicting frameworks — helpless on one hand, combative on the other —reinforce bias. One narrative minimises Indigenous women's agency; the other demonises those who do not conform to a submissive stereotype. Together, these constructions ignore the complexity and strength of Indigenous women and overlook self-efficacy, capability and individuality.

By examining the experiences of Indigenous women and families affected by violence, I show how institutions marginalise, ignore and speak over Indigenous women. This pattern of exclusion also appears in the broader discourse surrounding issues that matter to the Indigenous women and families who share their stories in this book. The chapters that follow continue to examine these exclusions and make clear why Indigenous women's voices must shape how violence is understood and responded to.

EXPLORING THE INFRASTRUCTURE OF VIOLENCE

> I think that the important thing to realise about torture is that every society, which includes Australia, the United Kingdom and the United States, has an infrastructure of violence, that has kept societies in the way they function to this day. (Holland 2018)

At this point, you may be wondering about the origin of this chapter's title, 'The infrastructure of violence'. The term was coined by former Zimbabwean politician Mrs Sekai Holland, whose advocacy and lived experiences profoundly inspired me. Mrs Holland defines the 'infrastructure of violence' as the systems and structures within society that enable or support violence in subtle but often unrecognised ways (Aedy 2018; Berzeg and Coello 2013; The Zimbabwean 2015). These systems encompass institutions and the individuals within them, which can normalise violent acts or render them acceptable in specific contexts. Consequently, acts of violence often go unchallenged or ignored. For instance, consider institutionalised strip searches, where an incarcerated person is required to remove clothing under the supervision of an employee of an institution such as a prison. While this is a standard procedure in a prison system, it can be deeply traumatising for those subjected to it. This example underscores how the infrastructure of violence operates within social systems, creating an environment where harmful practices persist without adequate scrutiny or acknowledgement.

I first met Mrs Holland, who I see as a change agent and an advocate for building peace, in 2016 when she visited the University of Newcastle and spoke about the violence and torture she endured after being arrested and held in police custody at the Harare Police Station in Zimbabwe in 2007. She was a politician at the time, lobbying for the rights of women during the Mugabe regime. The injuries she sustained included multiple broken bones and more than 80 lacerations, which required lengthy treatment in hospital. At the time, she was in her mid-sixties (Aedy 2018; Berzeg and Coello 2013; The Zimbabwean 2015). Despite this experience, Mrs Holland remained steadfast in her fight for human rights and peace building, continuing her work that included, in the 1970s, contributions to the Aboriginal Land Rights movement in Australia, where she assisted in establishing the children's service Murawina in Redfern's Aboriginal community.

Mrs Holland's words have stayed with me. Even to this day, when I reflect on her experiences, I struggle to understand how a woman who had been treated so inhumanly could look past the hurt and pain and work towards an agenda of peace. I find it difficult to think of anything worse than a grandmother being treated as Mrs Holland was. I remain in awe of her wisdom, her warmth, her beautiful smile, her giggle and her soft-spoken voice. While it took me some time to move through my thoughts, feelings and emotions when I heard about her experience, I came to realise what many survivors understand: there is life after violence.

Mrs Holland's experiences, shared through newspaper articles and radio interviews (Aedy 2018; Berzeg and Coello 2013; The Zimbabwean 2015), illustrate what her concept of the infrastructure of violence might entail and how individuals can move forward after experiencing violence. I build on her foundational ideas and acknowledge her as a catalyst for my own understanding and theorisation of this term.

My hope is to extend the concept of the infrastructure of violence, adding depth to its interpretation. In this book, I explore violence and its complexities, ranging across the micro and macro levels. Most importantly, I avoid viewing violence in isolation or as an isolated episodic occurrence. Violence should be recognised as existing along a continuum and manifesting in various forms — from individual incidents that may be relationship-specific to broader patterns that unfold between individuals, within communities and across systems and structures. A comprehensive framing of violence as a continuum allows for a more nuanced understanding of its pervasive nature.

Drawing on the research of Rodgers and O'Neill (2012), the concept of the infrastructure of violence can be seen to encompass physical structures in communities, including the planning and locations of these spaces. By applying a social engineering perspective to the physical environment, we can observe how community planning often reflects and reinforces social segregation (Rodgers and O'Neill 2012; Wacquant and Steinmetz 2009). Although not necessarily apparent, communities are strategically zoned based on affordability, resulting in systemic disparities (Rodgers and O'Neill 2012; Wacquant and Steinmetz 2009). For instance, lower-income individuals are typically concentrated in specific areas that have rental accommodation and social housing, while new housing developments featuring larger properties are often designed for wealthier residents. Societal structures determine who can reside where, largely influenced by economic circumstances and levels of affluence.

In the Australian context, disparities in physical infrastructure profoundly affect Indigenous peoples and perpetuate the social and political systems that historically inflicted violence on them. While housing initiatives designed to improve affordability and support first homebuyers may provide some support to Indigenous communities and families, many still rely on social or community housing. Often, they face the dual challenge of paying rent while grappling with affordability issues, further entrenching their vulnerability within the broader infrastructure of violence. This systemic inequity highlights the urgent need for more comprehensive approaches to address disparities in physical infrastructure (such as housing) that impact Indigenous populations.

Systemic inequities that reflect the broader infrastructure of violence disproportionately impact Indigenous women in Australia, whose experiences of marginalisation and vulnerability are exacerbated by socioeconomic disparities (Wacquant and Steinmetz 2009). By examining the specific challenges faced by Indigenous women, we can better understand how the interplay of sociopolitical factors and structural violence contributes to their experiences.

A key mechanism that keeps this infrastructure looking neutral is what I call *false equivalence.* A common logic used to describe conditions, false equivalence treats unequal conditions as though they are the same and then names the result as fairness. In practice, it sounds like: 'we treat everyone the same'. But sameness is not neutral when Indigenous women do not enter systems on equal ground. At the point of help-seeking, Indigenous women are at the cultural interface (Nakata 2007) with a service system where disbelief is racialised, surveillance histories shape interpretation, and disclosure risks triggering consequences across other systems beyond the violence itself. When a single credibility standard, a single risk threshold and a single behavioural script are applied to lives shaped by colonisation, Western institutional ideologies and ongoing control, inequality is reproduced while appearing impartial. False equivalence is not a misunderstanding; it is one of the operating logics of the infrastructure of violence.

The women's stories in this book tell of their experiences of multiple forms of violence — including state-based violence and violence perpetrated by individuals (such as intimate partners, friends and family members). Some have experienced violence from state employees. None of the women I spoke to experienced violence perpetrated by a stranger. This does not preclude violence from strangers; it simply illustrates that, in these stories, the violent person was known to the women.

How and *why* do these experiences happen? If we can answer this, we can begin to develop improved responses in moments of crisis while also acknowledging that Indigenous women experience violence in a way that is different from non-Indigenous women.

PRESENT AND ACTIVE – THE RISK OF DEFINING WOMEN AS RESILIENT

It's important to realise that people who experience violence are still actively present in their own lives. This concept is highlighted by Martin Nakata (2007:208), who emphasises that Torres Strait Islanders have always been 'actors in their own present'. Despite colonisation through specific methods of imposed regulation, Torres Strait Islanders were always active participants in their historical moments, not passive victims. Their engagement is exemplified by events like the Torres Strait Maritime Strike of 1936, a significant act of resistance against oppressive colonial control that saw Islanders refusing to work on the pearling boats which were controlled by the Queensland Government.

Torres Strait Islander people have experienced different methods of imposed regulation to those experienced by Aboriginal communities. But in similar ways, through various forms of activism and protest, Aboriginal people across Australia have resisted the power structures imposed on them. This concept of being active agents also applies to Indigenous women who experience violence, and their responses detailed in the following chapters demonstrate remarkable strength and awareness. These women were acutely conscious of the violence and the potential for further violence in their relationships and developed an ability to assess situations. They learned to read situations and anticipate any escalation in behaviour. This awareness underscores their agency, illustrating that they are not merely passive victims of their circumstances but individuals who navigate and challenge the complexities of their relationships.

Many women who experience violence must fight for their survival. Some lose their lives in the process — as shared by some families in this book. I wish these stories were fictional, but they are not. They demonstrate the violence these women experienced and how their families' lives were changed forever. These women have endured violence in relationships and from systems — including violence perpetuated by individuals who are mandated to serve and protect the community. Their stories are one part of their journeys.

Defining Indigenous women and families as resilient risks discrediting them. In some cases a woman must overcome or survive conditions that prevent her leaving a violent partner. She might need to ensure her own safety and that of children and family members — perhaps understanding the likely violence or potential threat to others if she attempts to leave a volatile relationship (or even expresses an intent to leave). Such experiences can force women to experience violence as a necessity. And in these moments, many Indigenous women draw on their inner survival and hope. It's difficult to understand that, at this interface, women can experience inner survival and hope. To outsiders, it's easy to dismiss the woman's agency and ignore the profound power and control wielded by the violent person. In these moments, the women do not experience resilience. This is survival.

Society tends to oversimplify lived experiences, especially when Indigenous women have endured violence. Violence is not simple. For Indigenous women, it is frequently complicated by historical factors and multigenerational experiences of trauma — making the violence cumulative and compounded. Oversimplifying violence can tell a community-wide story of violent acts or statistics, but it cannot encapsulate the story of who the women are, how they live their lives, their life histories and their experiences with children and families. When we frame a survivor's experiences through the lens of resilience, we risk manufacturing a reductionist view that inadvertently removes the woman's agency and ignores that she is an active participant in her own life — a woman who is navigating hostile and violent environments and experiences.

WHAT IS VIOLENCE?

Violence has many meanings and can be interpreted subjectively. From my knowledge and understanding, violence is any action, behaviour or process that causes harm, either with intention to hurt or not. Violence is in behaviours and the ways people speak to each other. It can include words and tone of voice. It can include what is not said.

The women who contribute to this book provide a range of views about what constitutes violence:

> I suppose it would be ... many different factors, so whether it be physical, verbal, mental, financial, I suppose it's individually dealing with violence, interpersonal. (**Malia**)

> So violence between people can be directed but it can be indirect and it can just be ... violence isn't just all physical. So much of my domestic violence was physical and so much of it was emotional but it was directed at me being told that I wasn't good enough, I wasn't anything. I'd never amount to anything, my family was shit, I was just a piece of shit and isolating me from people, I find that to be violence as well. It all just sort of ... all those little things all coming together, then the physical violence on top of that, that's my understanding. (**Kima**)

> It's violence inflicted on someone that can't defend themselves ... and it comes in forms of emotional, verbal and physical violence. (**Anika**)

> Violence is like yelling at someone even; to me, like, I know that it took me a long time to be able to go into shopping centres because I thought every man was going to punch me in the head. (**Lenna**)

> There's been different violence in my life. I'm 41 and I would say ... my earliest memories ... have been very traumatic. With my parents,

> witnessing violence from my father and what he did to my mother. My parents were in the front seat of the car and my sister and I in the back seat and they're arguing and I can remember my father threatening to drive us off the cliff. I also remember him beating my mum pretty bad around the front yard and me trying to stop my sister from seeing it. But also as a child, I experienced sexual abuse at the same time by a different person. (**Jaylah**)

Much of the violence the women experienced combined different forms of violence — emotional, psychological, verbal, physical, financial, sexual and what we now call coercive control. Their experiences differed: some women experienced physical violence from the very beginning of a relationship, while others experienced a process of grooming that, on reflection, they identified as violence that was hidden early in their relationships through tactics of manipulation and intimidation. Several women experienced violence from multiple partners and family members.

The stories in this book are all examples of domestic or family violence. The most common type of violence told in the stories is a form of 'intimate terrorism', with coercive control being the method most often employed by the perpetrator (Johnson 2008; Stark 2013). At times, patterns of violence support repetitive patterns of help-seeking behaviour by survivors (Johnson 2008; Stark 2013). Some of the women describe a cycle of violence and help-seeking in which they repeatedly left and then went back (or took the person back). Few women spoke about violence as a form of resistance, though some describe times when they resisted violence by attempting to be violent themselves — in these situations, violence became a mechanism of self-defence.

> It was just this cycle, it just went on and on, but I thought it would get better and you listen to so many people, [they] say that it's never going to get better, but I thought I was different and I thought he was

> different and then gradually over time I became isolated. He started putting down all my friends ... If I wasn't at work, [he said] I was sleeping with people and all these accusations, it was just easier to not associate with anyone or go anywhere because I knew I was going to cop it when I got home. So, then I found myself really isolated with no friends. I just went to work, and I came home. I stayed with him for a few years, and he ended up breaking my jaw and fracturing my skull and smashing my teeth and other, just say, like sexual, stuff. It got bad. I didn't have much contact with my family, just kind of me and him, we moved away for a bit. Got really isolated and I was just sort of finding the strength to leave him, I don't think I would have, if I didn't find out that I was pregnant. (**Malia**)

The voices of the women show that violence is an act that causes harm to another person, or to people, animals or property, either deliberately or indirectly. Violence makes another person feel unsafe. At the very least, it makes them check their surroundings to ensure their safety. This is not an exhaustive description of violence, nor does it describe all types of violence. However, it provides context for discussing the phenomenon of violence.

A formal description of violence might look like this: violence is the absence of peace, the deprivation of a person's needs or freedom, it limits an individual's personal growth and can be acted out by individuals, groups, systems or structures (Galtung 1969, 1990, 1998; Heise 1998; Parsons 2001). Violence can be intentional or unintentional, through conscious or unconscious actions, and can include rationalisation and justification through cognitive dissonance. Violence can even be legalised and legislated (Moreton-Robinson 2000; Rodgers and O'Neill 2012; Parsons 2001; Moses et al. 2004; Hunter 1993). It can be physical, psychological, financial or spiritual. Violence can occur with or without objects and weapons, which can be obvious or hidden and concealed

(Galtung 1969, 1990, 1998; Heise 1998; Parsons 2001). The typologies of violence can differ, as can its methods, which can be direct, cultural or structural (Galtung 1969, 1990, 1998; Heise 1998; Parsons 2001). A whole infrastructure ensures violence is seen, perceived and understood — sometimes knowingly, sometimes not. Together, this creates an infrastructure of violence.

Differentiating Indigenous women's experience of violence

Defining the way Indigenous women experience violence is important because it includes layers of complexity that may be overlooked or not fully understood by (among others) witnesses and services that respond to calls for help. What makes the experience different for Indigenous women is that typologies of violence extend the spheres in which violence and harm can be perpetrated. When Indigenous women discuss violence, the discussion almost always includes intersectional factors of race, racism, sexism, ableism and multiple subordinations (Crenshaw 1989, 1991). These discussions can further burden the survivor, who must deal with discrimination while seeking assistance, reporting violence and preparing themselves emotionally to retell their trauma (Cullen, Mackean, Longbottom et al. 2022; Cullen, Mackean, Walker et al. 2022). The women I spoke with said they felt judged, and some felt unable to approach service providers because of their awareness of individual and societal stereotypes about Indigenous women.

Many Indigenous women fear the places where violence is disclosed. This fear is compounded by the threat of child removal, which can occur following mandatory reporting.

> The amount of stress and the emphasis on the women, if police come and there's domestic violence, you're a bad mother, you're a bad woman, child protection might come and take your kids and all that sort of business. (**Keira**)

When they disclose violent incidents, Indigenous women will often disclose other types of violence and speak about the discrimination they have encountered when attempting to seek help (Cullen, Mackean, Longbottom et al. 2022; Cullen, Mackean, Walker et al. 2022). This is where invisible cultural and structural violence can occur (Galtung 1969, 1990, 1998; Heise 1998; c 2001).

REFUSING TO BE WHITE

In discussing Indigenous women's perceptions of violence, I want to make it clear that Indigenous women do not want to be white women — well, at least, not the ones I have spoken to and know. Most Indigenous women do not require the push for gender equity or the rights framework that many white women seek — because, in Indigenous communities, we typically already live in an egalitarian way. Women are part of the social structure, and we make significant contributions to communities and our families (Moreton-Robinson 2000; Bunda 2020).

Indigenous women have always provided food, cared for their families and nurtured communities in their own distinct ways. In my experience, Indigenous women continue to enact our rights and we refuse to accept the additional identities by which feminism in particular attempts to contain and confine us (Moreton-Robinson 2000; Nakata 2007; hooks 1982). In the context of this book, women and families refuse to be quiet, refuse to be made invisible and refuse to be seen as victims.

Indigenous womanhood is not synonymous with white womanhood — which is closely tied to the illegal occupation of invasion — nor is it akin to that of migrants and refugee women. While non-white women may have a connection with Indigenous women through experiences of racism, their connection to the nation of Australia differs from that of Indigenous women. Indigenous women experience womanhood as being grounded in a timeless connection to land, sea and cosmologies. We understand the ever-present, self-determining processes of communal responsibility and accountability, and can never be disconnected from this, even in the current day. Indigenous womanhood is grounded in subjectivities that are informed by Indigenous understandings and values and based on communal connections (Moreton-Robinson 2000).

It is crucial to acknowledge that, at times, white women have been complicit in the violence perpetrated against Indigenous women. This complicity can manifest in many ways, including the perpetuation of stereotypes, the support of systems that marginalise voices and the failure to confront injustices faced by Indigenous women. Recognising this complicity is essential for understanding the broader dynamics of oppression and for fostering solidarity and accountability in the fight for justice for Indigenous women. I return to this concept in the next chapter.

The work of bell hooks (1982) shows that the ideology of superiority and inferiority is reinforced by systemic and structural influences that shape society's perceptions of victimhood. These influences determine who is recognised as a 'worthy victim' deserving protection, while simultaneously misidentifying others as less worthy or non-ideal. At times, those who survive violence are even categorised as perpetrators. From the perspective of Indigenous women, these intersecting dynamics reveal the complexities of their experiences and highlight how specific narratives and systemic inequities contribute to marginalisation. Understanding this perspective is crucial for developing a more nuanced approach to addressing violence against Indigenous women and ensuring our voices are heard in discussions about prevention, interventions, support and justice.

SELF-DETERMINATION AND AGENCY

Self-determination can mean different things to different people. For me, it signifies the ability to make personal decisions about things that affect my life. Self-determination includes both the decision-making process and the capacity to act on those decisions. Achieving self-efficacy and mastery over one's life are significant outcomes of embracing the principles of self-determination (Simpson 2014, 2016; Nakata and Nakata 2022; Rademaker and Rowse 2020).

In legal and governmental contexts, the interpretation and application of self-determination varies, encompassing both individual and collective dimensions. In international law, self-determination is often associated with the collective rights of Indigenous peoples — it empowers Indigenous communities to make decisions about their lives without external interference (Deci and Ryan 2012; Kirzner and Miserandino 2023). In this way, self-determination serves as a cornerstone in the Indigenous rights movement, affirming the autonomy and agency of communities managing their affairs (Rademaker and Rowse 2020; Nakata 2015).

The international law perspective shows that Indigenous people have the right to govern their lands, resources and cultural practices, and typically emphasises the group or collective rights of communities (Rademaker and Rowse 2020). In contrast, self-determination theory usually applies a psychological lens to explore factors that motivate self-determination at the individual level (Deci and Ryan 2012; Kirzner and Miserandino 2023). From this perspective, self-determination relates to individual agency, autonomy, relatedness and competence (Deci and Ryan 2012; Kirzner and Miserandino 2023). Martin Nakata's work on self-efficacy and self-attainment provides a relevant model here, which can be understood as a mechanism to support Indigenous women who leave violence and need support (Nakata 2007; Nakata and Nakata 2022). Adding to the constructs of autonomy, relatedness and competence, Nakata extends this with agency that links to self-efficacy and self-determination (Nakata and Nakata 2022).

Kima's story is an example of self-determination and agency. Once she discovered she was pregnant, Kima felt motivated to act. In an act of resistance and an act of self-determination, she began to hide money which made it possible to leave the perpetrator.

> I was pregnant, and I stayed with him for the first bit and kept working and saved up enough money. I had to hide my money in a torch that had no batteries in it, it was the only way I could hide money where he wouldn't steal it for his pot ... As soon as I had enough money saved up I got us a house, I got away from him and everything was okay until he found out where I was living. (**Kima**)

Agency is closely linked to self-determination. I'm particularly drawn to Indigenous scholarship that emphasises agency as the ability of individuals to exert control over their lives (Nakata and Nakata 2022; Nakata 2015). The stories in this book demonstrate women and families as agents of their own lives. Despite challenges, they exhibited a remarkable degree of control and agency by resisting violence and navigating a complex, hostile environment until they could make a decisive change in their circumstances.

I've adopted the concept of agency described by Martin Nakata and Vicky Nakata (2022) in their work on student success, which builds on the work of psychologist Albert Bandura (2006) in the area of human development, adaptation and change. Drawing on social-cognitive theory, they show that self-efficacy and mastery are key outcomes in striving for student success — and I believe they also apply when supporting Indigenous women who seek to leave violent relationships. Both agency and self-efficacy involve self-regulation and recognising that it's possible to move beyond current circumstances. In this book, Indigenous women show how they challenge and 'speak back' to prevailing discourses. This focus highlights their perception of themselves and their responses to specific situations. It demonstrates their agency (Nakata 2007; Nakata and Nakata 2022; Nakata 2015).

RESTORATION OF POWER

In her book *Mohawk Interruptus*, Audra Simpson introduces the concept of the restoration of power and prompts deeper inquiry into how acts of self-determination can manifest in Indigenous people's right to refuse the narratives and roles inscribed for them (Simpson 2014). In this context, the restoration of power frames our understanding of the violence faced by Indigenous women and highlights their active involvement in surviving and strategising to leave life-threatening situations. This demonstrates their strength and shows that life beyond violence is not merely about surviving — it's about thriving.

Lenna described the difficulty of being in a relationship and planning to leave. Her motivation was based on a belief that she would improve the lives of herself and her children.

> I love my kids. They are strong. I was broken, but I had to survive to escape. I couldn't let him break me. I just did what I needed and pretended. It took years to escape the most violent trauma. It's not easy being something you are not. Being someone else to live and survive. (**Lenna**)

My work extends the idea of the restoration of power and links it with themes from Indigenous scholars, my own personal experience and the experiences of the women and families I interviewed. I aim to shift the accepted victim paradigm and ensure Indigenous women's voices and experiences are centred through acts of resistance and reclamation.

Restoration of power through resistance means that women 'speak back' against perpetrators of violence and against the systems and services that fail to support them and meet their needs (Simpson 2016). This type of resistance is complex. When Indigenous women leave violent situations, they need to navigate systemic challenges while striving to keep their families intact. They may face threats from child protection authorities alerted by mandatory reporters such as police and teachers, or they may face legal difficulties or financial concerns. Despite these obstacles, the stories in this book highlight women's resistance and assertive responses, as well as their refusal to accept a victim narrative, which is a recurring theme (including in Jemila's and Jaylah's stories).

Many Indigenous women refuse to accept the label of victim. Simpson (2014, 2016) emphasises the rights of Indigenous peoples to refuse assimilation into colonial frameworks, a stance that challenges dominant societal norms and formal structures. By rejecting the victim narrative, Indigenous women dismantle the associations of helplessness and hopelessness often ascribed to victimhood.

Indigenous scholarship highlights that the historical responsibility of Indigenous women to provide for their families and communities (Moreton-Robinson 2000; Maynard 2007; Hunter 1993) is critical to the continuity and advancement of Indigenous futures (Moreton-Robinson 2000; Nakata 2007; Fredericks 2008, 2010). It is within this framework that social justice processes integrate Indigenous scholarship to address the inequalities faced by Indigenous women, especially in the context of violence and their interactions with service sectors tasked with protection and support.

CHAPTER 2

THE INTERSECTION OF RACE, GENDER AND COLONIAL HISTORY

It's about understanding that as Indigenous women we've always been strong, we've always had a place in society which is different to the white Western world. We were never objects of possession, particularly not in my community, and, as I understand prior to contact, there were women that were stolen from other tribes. But if you did something like that and you got caught, payback was usually death; there was a big risk in doing stuff like that. But in terms of who we are as women today, there's power in all our stories and I think [an] understanding that there is a place and a space for Indigenous women — specifically, to tell our stories, of the erasing of our stories and our voice, because people think that they can talk about us in ways in which they think they're helping but it's not helping. And white women do that, white women in particular think that they can speak on our behalf. I think that we must have our own space to be able to talk and tell our own stories from the angle that we want to talk. They need to step back and just let us do what we need to do. (**Jaylah**)

I AM THE GRANDDAUGHTER OF THE ANCESTORS THAT GENOCIDE COULDN'T KILL

I start this section by reflecting on a day that evokes profound emotional turmoil for many Indigenous people: 26 January. Around this date in 1788, the First Fleet invaded what is now known as New South Wales, leading to widespread death and disease among the Indigenous community. One year, as I made my way to the annual Survival Day rally in Sydney, I felt a familiar tension and tiredness in my body—like a visceral reminder of the trauma my community has endured. Some social commentators argue that individuals like me 'choose' to feel this way—and through this they suggest that I am responsible for my emotional response. I often dismiss such comments, particularly when they come from other Indigenous people who, in my view, have become numb to their experiences or have rationalised the invasion through a process of cognitive dissonance. Trauma is processed in various ways, and there is no single 'right' approach to dealing with it.

On days like 26 January, my emotions fluctuate. Sometimes I feel anger, and at times I seek solitude and reflection. I am reminded of the wisdom of Audre Lorde (2007:130), who stated, 'Caring for myself is not self-indulgence, it is self-preservation, and that is an act of political warfare.' Lorde's comment informs my practice of self-care, leading me to step back from emotional engagement during significant racial discussions.

For many Indigenous people, 26 January is a day of both mourning and survival. It serves as an opportunity to honour our ancestors and acknowledge our collective pain. It is also a reminder of our survival, which I've captured in the title of this section, 'I am the granddaughter of the ancestors that genocide couldn't kill'.

I am proud of my Aboriginal heritage. For me, despite having fair skin, navigating the spaces outside my community has always been challenging. I have encountered discrimination and assumptions about my identity, often leading others to question 'what part' of me is Indigenous. I often encounter curiosity from people who misidentify me as

Polynesian, Māori or Latina, which I recognise as a social fascination with my perceived proximity to whiteness, or lack thereof. During a medical procedure, a radiographer asked me, 'So you're Māori?', when my chart clearly stated that I am Aboriginal. I have grown to accept that my appearance may confuse others. At an airport in San Francisco, a gentleman assumed my ethnicity and spoke to me in Spanish. His assumption, while surprising, highlights how people navigate societal classifications by categorising others based on appearance rather than acknowledging their identity. I was not considered white, but neither was I clearly Aboriginal. My responses differ in these moments, depending on who is making the comments and how tired I am.

I was raised in a family that instilled pride in my heritage and encouraged me to embrace my identity. The Longbottom family fostered an environment of acceptance without the pressure to quantify our Aboriginal heritage. In Indigenous culture, relationships often begin with questions that build connections, such as, 'Who is your mob?' or 'Where are you from?' This inquiry reflects a desire to connect with broader social and cultural networks, fostering a sense of community and belonging. It is also a framing to place someone, given how our communities are interconnected across the country — someone usually knows someone or is related somehow.

As I ventured beyond my family and community, I encountered persistent questions about my Indigenous identity. My biological parents are both Indigenous, with my mother's side proudly identifying as Aboriginal. My biological paternal family carries Aboriginal ancestry, but family members were raised white, with a family history of concealing their Aboriginal heritage.

BINARY CLASSIFICATIONS — AND LIVING IN THE DUALITY

Indigenous women face ongoing challenges in asserting their humanity while having to also educate others about who they are and what they experience. When they are met with material realities of racism, sexism and other forms of discrimination or aggression, it becomes necessary to show how they are perceived and compared to and against white women. Indigenous women often find themselves positioned outside the narrow frameworks imposed upon them. As Nakata (2007:195–196) explains, Indigenous people live within the cultural interface that is complex, multilayered and shaped by intersecting histories. This space exposes the limits of the binary classifications applied to Indigenous women — binaries juxtaposed against white womanhood that flattens the realities of their lives. Within this interface, Indigenous women are continually navigating dualities not of their own making, negotiating both how they are perceived and how they assert their identities.

At the cultural interface, false equivalence arrives as a demand for sameness, activating binary sorting — credible/unreliable, victim/perpetrator, compliant/non-compliant — so complexity reads as inconsistency, while guardedness or caution reads as non-compliance. There is an expectation that Indigenous women should be able to move through institutions as if history, race and surveillance do not shape outcomes. What is being measured is not only the woman's story but her conformity to an institutional script. False equivalence, enforced through these binaries, is how difference is erased at the interface while the system continues to look impartial. This binary does not occur in a vacuum; it is enabled by a hierarchy of womanhood in which Indigenous women are read against white norms, making othering the background condition on which false equivalence can operate at the cultural interface.

This enforcement looks objective precisely because credibility is read against white womanhood, as Moreton-Robinson (2000) shows, with Indigenous women routinely positioned outside of the benchmark. Following Nakata (2007), the point is not that women fit those binaries, but that we are compelled to perform legibility within them; Indigenous women — we — live through multiple intersecting identities that exceed the limits of those imposed frames. These identities also shape our lives as we navigate both the perceptions imposed on us and the knowledge produced about us.

Interpretations of Indigenous women are heavily influenced by the observer's viewpoint and the dominant societal constructs of womanhood that reflect Western perspectives. What I find interesting is that Indigenous women become visible only at particular moments, and it is this selective visibility that contributes to the complex landscape of Indigenous womanhood. Moments of visibility can quickly turn into invisibility (Huggins 1995; Johnson 2016; McGrath 1984, 1990; Robert 2001). This duality complicates the understanding of Indigenous womanhood, particularly regarding who is recognised and afforded protection against violence when it's inflicted on Indigenous women's bodies. The shifting dynamic of visibility and invisibility, yet another binary, determines who is afforded protection and who is not, sitting alongside the binary of the ideal and non-ideal victim as discussed later in this chapter. Recognising these patterns brings into focus the layered realities Indigenous women navigate, highlighting both challenges and opportunities that emerge in their — our — communities.

From a Western perspective, the binary framework is rooted in Christian values of male and female, with concepts of womanhood in Australia revolving around behaviours, performance and actions defined predominantly by white women. This binary creates a framework that imposes an ideology of womanhood (influenced by loyalties to narrow perceptions of femininity) and impacts the everyday lives of Indigenous women, compelling them to navigate and code-switch — between their family and cultural identities, and the expectations imposed by mainstream society (Moreton-Robinson 2000). Indigenous women may appear visible in certain contexts but can quickly become invisible when they do not conform to Western ideals of womanhood. Whiteness dominates from a position of power and privilege as an invisible norm and unchallenged practice (Moreton-Robinson 2000, 2015). This logic continues to shape societal functioning in Australia, where Indigenous people are still under constant surveillance and Indigenous women are often inadequately protected.

Moreover, when Indigenous women raise concerns or advocate for their rights, their voices are frequently ignored, omitted or spoken over. The works of Indigenous women who have continuously articulated these messages serve as a powerful reminder of the need for Indigenous voices in these discussions. This chapter reflects on the contributions of some of these influential figures, women who claimed their space — often through force rather than invitation — such as Aileen Moreton-Robinson, Jackie Huggins, the women from the Aboriginal Land Rights movement of the 1970s, and early trailblazers who voiced their concerns as far back as the 1920s but have remained relatively unknown.

RACIALISED FIRST – THEN DEFINED BY GENDER

In yarning with women and families during the research for this book, rather than purposely delving into specific aspects of race, gender, sexuality, ableism and other identities, these themes naturally emerged, revealing thoughts and feelings of judgement rooted in racial and gendered perspectives. Jaylah offered an insightful reflection on her experiences:

> It's like everything is predicated on race. People think it's a gendered space, well no, that comes after race. First and foremost, you're Indigenous, secondly you're a woman, so those two things in themselves create a whole bunch of different issues depending on what you're going through and then you have those other things of classism, ableism and sexuality. All these types of things can actually impact and possibly be points of discrimination. (**Jaylah**)

While the intersections of Indigeneity and gender have been explored in literature, the discussions often lack an Indigenous women's perspective. When I was growing up, the Indigenous women in my life were strong, staunch, caring and nurturing figures — they were, and remain, formidable forces of power. Yet media and cinema often portray Indigenous women through a lens of negative stereotypes, depicting them as unable to save themselves or in need of rescuing and retraining to conform to Western constructs of womanhood. Examples include the historical movie *Jedda* (Chauvel 1955), the representation of women in Baz Luhrmann's (2008) movie *Australia*, and the caricatures produced by cartoonist Bill Leak from the 1980s to 2010s. These white observers' representations are framed by both men and women who position themselves as authoritative knowers (Huggins 1987; Smallacombe 2004).

As Indigenous women navigate our daily lives, we are simultaneously racialised and gendered (Moreton-Robinson 2000; Crenshaw 1991; Collins 1993). Our Indigeneity is constantly present, with racial descriptors imposed on us. I am repeatedly asked about what part (or proportion) of me is Aboriginal. White womanhood is spared such accounting; white women appear (in government documents, for example) simply as women. However, the moment we name whiteness out loud, suddenly the calm is over. By merely using a descriptor or inscription similar to those often used to describe Indigenous women and denote our difference, we risk being labelled as racist. This distinction highlights how white women are accepted as the normative definition of womanhood. Jaylah again poignantly captures this experience:

> I don't know what it's like to live in a white woman's world because I've never grown up in a white woman's world, so I don't speak from that point of view. I speak from my experience of being an Indigenous woman, from an Indigenous community, from an Indigenous family embedded in my community which comes back to me being strong in my identity. (**Jaylah**)

Indigenous women diverge from white women in the way they are situated within the white, heterosexual patriarchy that binds them to a male/

female binary and defines white women as submissive property of white men (Moreton-Robinson 2000; Fredericks 2010; Conor 2016; Haskins and Maynard 2005). While feminism challenges the patriarchy, it often operates within the framework of white possessive logic that continues to marginalise Indigenous women (Moreton-Robinson 2000, 2015).

White feminism frequently claims that all women share a homogeneous experience of womanhood (Moreton-Robinson 2000). However, as Jaylah suggests, race and racism can be obscured in the focus on gender. We need to recognise that Indigenous women are racialised first, before they are defined by gender. These discussions are not new; Indigenous women scholars have long critiqued the rights-based liberation narratives propagated by white women (Moreton-Robinson 2000, 2015; Huggins 1995). While there may be shared experiences between Indigenous and white women, race and class serve as primary axes of oppression that subjugate Indigenous women. The power dynamics are obscured by embedded social norms that continue to perpetuate systemic inequalities (Moreton-Robinson 2000, 2015; Crenshaw 1991; Collins 1993; hooks 1989; Moses et al. 2004).

INTERSECTIONALITY IN THE EARLY TWENTIETH CENTURY

Prior to contact with colonisers, Indigenous women were recognised and respected in their communities and played crucial roles in sustaining communities and participating in decision-making processes. Their essential roles in egalitarian social structures contrast starkly with contemporary marginalisation.

Colonisation and the disruption of Indigenous cultural practices transformed societal roles in a systemic shift that dictated hierarchical relationships and determined who held power over whom. But in the early twentieth century, Indigenous women like Mrs Annie Bowden from La Perouse in New South Wales and Mrs Anna Morgan from Victoria played significant roles in challenging the myths and representations of Indigenous peoples (Bowden, A 1922; The Morning Bulletin 1935; The Horsham Times 1935). They made substantial contributions to Indigenous political history, advocating for their communities amidst oppressive conditions. Newspaper articles from the 1920s and 1930s document their activism against the prevailing scientific racism and hegemonic whiteness that they and their families experienced.

Mrs Bowden and Mrs Morgan are among the earliest Indigenous women activists in the public sphere, advocating for the rights of Indigenous communities. They were active during an era of severe government control, with constant surveillance of Indigenous people's movements. In each state, Protection Acts directed Indigenous people's lives and imposed harsh penalties for resistance. Despite this, Mrs Bowden and Mrs Morgan advocated for social justice and sovereign rights. Their resistance underscores the need for a nuanced understanding of their roles in the broader feminist movement.

Mrs Bowden takes on a white anthropologist

In 1922 Mrs Annie Bowden responded in the *Sydney Morning Herald* to an article by Daisy Bates titled 'Indigenous communism'. She refuted Bates's claims about Indigenous language, culture, violence, coming-of-age ceremonies and alleged acts of cannibalism. She critically analysed Bates's distortions and questioned the credibility of her sources, and began by emphasising her own credibility:

> Will you allow me, through the columns of your valuable paper, to reply to an article by Mrs. Daisy M. Bates, appearing in your issue of the 6th instant, re aboriginal communism ... It would be laughable if it were not so serious; and we know it is not true. I am an aboriginal, and understand and speak eight different languages. I am an educated woman, having been educated in the State schools of Victoria, and I think that I am in a better position to know than a white woman. (Bowden 1922)

Mrs Bowden countered Bates's allegation about mistreatment of Indigenous women with her own lived experiences:

> I was always kindly treated, and the unkindness Mrs. Bates so graphically describes is surely of some other nation. The women were always taken care of in my case, and made much of, and there was more discipline in the camps than there is in many white homes to-day. The aboriginals had their own government; the law was binding, and anyone breaking that law was punished by death. If a young man wanted to marry a girl it had to be approved of by the leaders there, and no one girl, or one man, ever got a wife in any other way. Boys were taught from earliest infancy to respect their mother and their sisters ... (Bowden 1922)

Furthermore, Mrs Bowden (1922) clarified that issues requiring correction typically involved parents rather than children, dispelling Bates's fantastical notions surrounding witchcraft: 'If there was an act of disobedience, it was the parents who were dealt with, not the children.'

In refuting claims of cannibalism, Mrs Bowden questioned what Bates could know about initiation ceremonies, which were reserved for select attendees:

> If, as Mrs. Bates says, they were such cannibals there, and they killed and ate people for the smallest offence, how is it that she was allowed to witness so dreadful a scene, without being eaten herself? Initiation as I know it was a sacred rite, and no one but a select few were ever allowed to witness it ... It was an utter impossibility for anyone outside the selected circle, so how Mrs. Bates comes to know so much about initiation I cannot tell ... As for skinning their babies for water-bags, an aboriginal woman would never do it; she is too fond of her baby. (Bowden 1922)

Mrs Bowden's letter demonstrates an early attempt to challenge colonial narratives. Mrs Bowden belonged to the Australian Aboriginal Progressive Association, which aimed to reclaim power for Indigenous communities. As the association's political efforts gained momentum, it faced escalating repression from the state and was ultimately forced to disband (Maynard 2007).

Mrs Morgan advocates for Indigenous women in the 1930s

In 1935 another Indigenous woman, Mrs Anna Morgan, spoke out against injustices faced by Indigenous people. She delivered a powerful address at a women's rally in Melbourne on International Women's Day in February, advocating for equal pay, improved children's conditions and support for unemployed women (The Morning Bulletin 1935; The Horsham Times 1935).

Mrs Morgan's position as an Elder and an Aboriginal woman at a rally predominantly attended by white women is mirrored in rallies we see today. Her advocacy raised critical issues that were overlooked by the rally's main agenda, which centred on equity in pay for white women at a time when Indigenous women like Mrs Morgan were ineligible for welfare payments, as the *Aborigines Protection Act* allowed state governments to withhold funds (Murphy 2013). Furthermore, despite being elderly, Mrs Morgan could not access the aged pension, as Aboriginal people were considered wards of the state and excluded from the pension, which had been legislated in 1908 (The Morning Bulletin 1935; The Horsham Times 1935; Murphy 2013). Although activist William Cooper lobbied for their inclusion in 1936, it took until 1941 for change to happen — and even then Aboriginal people could only receive the pension if they applied through the Aboriginal Protection Board (The Morning Bulletin 1935; The Horsham Times 1935; Murphy 2013).

The 1935 rally aimed to elevate the status of women — that is, white women — and issues facing Indigenous women were largely ignored. At the time of the rally, many Aboriginal women worked in domestic service for white families, and they were often subjected to violence and exploitation by the men of these households (Moreton-Robinson 2000; Maynard 2007; Conor 2016; Haskins and Maynard 2005). Mrs Morgan seized the opportunity to expose the dire situation facing all Indigenous people, not just women. Described in the press as an 'educated [Indigenous] woman, who had never spoken previously at any similar rally' (The Morning Bulletin 1935), she was likely one of the first people to publicly address white audiences on the plight of Indigenous communities. As *The Morning Bulletin* (1935) reported, Mrs Morgan poignantly stated:

> What is the position of aboriginal women? ... I am not allowed the old-age pension because I am 'too dark'. I get nothing from the Aboriginal Protection Board because my mother was a half-caste. What are we? Can anyone tell us what we are? Not allowed to vote, not allowed to own the land which was all ours before the white people came.
>
> There is no sanctity for our women. In the settlements the boss has absolute power. He can separate a man from his wife and children for weeks, if he likes.
>
> Our children are not getting the same education as the white children. The teachers sent out are not always properly qualified, and do not bother to teach anything beyond the three R's. In one case a girl became fully qualified and was not allowed to teach children of her own race, because she is an aboriginal. Missionaries who come to the settlement send their own children to college on what they earn at this, but do they ever think that some poor aboriginal child might benefit from an education? Is there a single case on record where they have tried sending such a child to college? No.
>
> You white people complain of sustenance. The poor black has been on sustenance all his life. There is no butter, and very little

> meat, fish, or vegetables in the ration handed out to the aboriginals in the settlements.
>
> The girls are taken by force from the settlements as soon as they reach the age of 14, so that they will not marry back into the black race and perpetuate it. They are sent out to service, which is very little different from slavery, in white families. This is because the Board wants to stamp out the aboriginal race. (The Morning Bulletin 1935)

Throughout her speech, Mrs Morgan discussed several intersecting issues affecting Indigenous women, many of which remain relevant today —the exclusion of Indigenous women from financial assistance, disparities in educational opportunities, the lack of voting rights and land ownership, the threat of violence and separation under the authority of mission managers, and food insecurity and provisions typical in missions and reserves. Her courageous address highlighted the plight of Indigenous women and placed their struggles in a broader framework of intersectional oppression. Her comments reveal the critical lack of acknowledgement of Indigenous women's issues within predominantly white feminist movements.

In her concluding remarks, Mrs Morgan emphasised the importance of solidarity among all workers and the need for unity in the fight for Indigenous rights (The Morning Bulletin 1935). Her insights show how Indigenous women were relegated to second-class citizenship, with their struggles often overshadowed by the concerns of white women. As noted by scholars such as bell hooks (1982), Patricia Hill Collins (1993) and Aileen Moreton-Robinson (2015), there are clear differences between white feminism, which centres on rights for white women, and Indigenous feminism, which emphasises responsibility to self and community. Mrs Morgan's activism calls attention to multilayered forms of oppression faced by Indigenous women — issues that continue to require advocacy and visibility in contemporary discourse.

UNDERSTANDING DIFFERENCES: INDIGENOUS WOMEN'S VOICES IN THE 1960S AND 1970S

The 1960s and 1970s were pivotal decades in Australia, marked by the emergence of the Aboriginal Black Power movement and the push for land rights. The period also illustrates the different struggles faced by Indigenous women compared to their white counterparts. The documentary *Ningla A-Na* (Cavadini 1972) captures key moments from this era, including significant events related to the Black Power movement and the Aboriginal Tent Embassy in Canberra in 1972, where many demonstrators were Indigenous women.

In a notable exchange in the documentary, Indigenous women Alana Doolan and Isabel Coe engage in a conversation with unnamed white feminists about the Indigenous political movement and the role of Indigenous women within it. The dialogue underscores critical issues that white feminists often overlook. Ms Doolan asserts the strength of black women, stating, 'Black women have always been strong; sexually, emotionally, mentally, more so than the black man ... Most of the men now, the black men, wouldn't be where they are today if it weren't for the black woman' (Cavadini 1972). Ms Coe highlights the omnipresent violence faced by Indigenous people, commenting, 'Blacks are going through violence every day of their lives, and you women just talk about liberating women' (Cavadini 1972). Her comment brings attention to the urgency of Indigenous issues compared to the trajectory of white women's liberation.

The white feminist perspective emerges when one participant claims, 'Blacks need to liberate themselves; we can't liberate you' (Cavadini 1972). Ms Coe counters by emphasising the need for solidarity: 'We can't afford to split at the moment. We can't liberate without your support', and further urges the white women to 'educate your own people about our problems and our struggles' (Cavadini 1972). Ms Doolan expresses frustration with the lack of tangible support from white feminists, observing,

'I don't know what women's liberation has done for the black people here in Australia' (Cavadini 1972).

Ningla A-Na highlights the misalignment of priorities between white feminists and Indigenous women. The Indigenous women emphasise their unique positioning in society and the vital support they provide to Indigenous men. Many Indigenous communities adhere to matrilineal bloodlines, representing a stark contrast to the patriarchal structures prevalent in other communities.

While both Indigenous and white women experience gender-based subjugation, their respective liberation movements differ in purpose. Ms Coe highlights the prevalence of violence in Indigenous communities, pointing out that while white feminists call for Indigenous self-liberation, it is systemic neoliberalism and white possessive logics that perpetuate Indigenous women's oppression.

White feminists' insistence that Indigenous people must liberate themselves does not recognise the interconnected but separate struggles of Indigenous men and women. As Ms Coe notes, Indigenous women cannot separate themselves from Indigenous men due to the shared experiences of racism (Cavadini 1972). This mutual oppression necessitates collective action. The white feminist movement often seeks separation from men based on rights, while the Indigenous women's movement emphasises inclusivity and community responsibility (Moreton-Robinson 2000). The contemporary Indigenous liberation movement reflects the egalitarian frameworks that operated prior to colonisation and uses a responsibility model that advocates for the collective liberation of all Indigenous people. The conversation in *Ningla A-Na* illustrates the critical misunderstandings that can arise in feminist discourse. For Indigenous women, liberation is a communal responsibility born from shared struggles, while for white feminists it is often about individual rights and separation from male oppression. Understanding these differences is essential for fostering genuine support and allyship between movements.

The authority to speak: the Bell–Huggins debate

The Bell–Huggins debate, highlighted in Moreton-Robinson's (2000) book *Talkin' up to the white woman*, examines the speaking positions of white women who assert themselves as authoritative voices on issues affecting Indigenous women and communities. This debate emerged in 1989 when Diane Bell, a white anthropologist, published an article, 'Speaking about rape is everyone's business', in *Women's Studies International Forum* (Bell and Nelson 1989). Bell claimed that rape in Indigenous communities was a universal concern and asserted her authority to speak on the matter, citing permission from her co-author, Topsy Napurrula Nelson. Notably, the article lacked survivor testimonies, a significant oversight (Moreton-Robinson 2000, 2003).

In response, Indigenous women — including Dr Jackie Huggins, Professor Aileen Moreton-Robinson and Dr Jo Willmot — protested Bell's article, arguing that she assumed the role of 'knower' while speaking on behalf of Indigenous women (Moreton-Robinson 2000, 2003). During the Australian anthropology conference in Adelaide the following year, they openly questioned Bell's methods and assumptions. However, their concerns were dismissed, and they were characterised by the predominantly white audience as being 'angry' and 'ungrateful' (Moreton-Robinson 2000, 2003). They were further labelled as 'aggressive, emotional and hostile', reinforcing the stereotype of the angry black woman (Griffin 2012).

Despite decades of Indigenous women's activism and advocacy, white women continue to dominate the discourse about violence against Indigenous women (Moreton-Robinson 2000; Smallacombe 2004). In our conversation, Jaylah articulated this tension:

> White women in particular think that they can speak on our behalf. I think that we must have our own space to be able to talk and tell our own stories from the angle that we want to talk and what we want to share. White women must understand that they need to step back.

> They need to step back and just let us do what we need to do, we might be all women but at the end of the day, Indigenous women need that space specifically. (**Jaylah**)

Indigenous women are inherently best positioned to address the issues that affect them, yet they often find their voices marginalised or silenced. Figures like Annie Bowden, Anna Morgan, Isabel Coe, Alana Doolan, Jackie Huggins and Aileen Moreton-Robinson have been pivotal in creating platforms for Indigenous women's voices. Today, Indigenous women assert their narratives independently, emphasising their capability to speak for themselves without white intermediaries. While allyship can be valuable, it must not overshadow Indigenous women's own voices. As Dr Sonia Smallacombe (2004) states, 'it seems that someone has claimed the space to speak on Indigenous violence and that space does not necessarily belong to Indigenous women'.

Indigenous women continue to discuss strategies to address violence in our communities, yet our contributions are often disregarded. This reveals a persistent pattern of narrative controls — about who is recognised as 'knower' and who is permitted to speak about critical issues. Despite the legacies of past advocates, many contemporary Indigenous voices are still silenced in academic forums, public discussions and government agendas surrounding violence in Indigenous communities. As the debate continues, it remains vital to challenge who occupies the space to speak and ensure that Indigenous women have the autonomy to narrate our own experiences and advocate for our communities.

THE ONGOING CRISIS OF VIOLENCE AND THE MATRIX OF DOMINATION

In Australia little has been accomplished to mitigate the violence, rape and sexual assault experienced by Indigenous women and girls. We continue to face significant barriers in accessing services established to support survivors of sexual violence. As I discuss in 'Refusing to be white' in Chapter 1, Indigenous women cannot be categorised alongside other multicultural groups and, further, white women have historically been complicit in violence against Indigenous women — a reality that persists to this day, even among self-professed allies to the Indigenous cause. While Indigenous women work to assert our agency and right to safety, many white women adopt a rights-based approach that overlooks the specific impacts of these rights on Indigenous women.

This issue is further complicated by the tendency of white women to presume they know what is best for all women. While not dismissing the intentions of allies, we need to critique actions that appear supportive but perpetuate inequalities. For instance, some white women organise rallies and invite Indigenous women to deliver a Welcome to Country or Acknowledgement of Country, which is then followed by sharing personal stories of surviving trauma. However, this approach raises questions about what happens next. Many white women return to their own agendas, centred on their own rights, while, for Indigenous women, little changes.

The complexities of Indigenous women's experiences illustrate the need for a nuanced understanding of intersectionality in any discussion about gender and violence. True allyship must recognise Indigenous women's autonomy and commit to addressing our specific needs — beyond surface-level inclusion.

Multiple domains of power contribute to the oppression of Indigenous women in Australia. We confront violence in everyday life, at interpersonal, community and structural levels. This hierarchical logic, which hooks (2015:36) identifies as central to Western domination, also underpins the racialised positioning of Indigenous women described by Moreton-Robinson (2000:288).

British invaders viewed the white race as superior and 'civilised', leading to the appropriation of land and resources and forcing Indigenous people into conditions of dispossession, displacement, servitude and enslavement. Today, the ideology of white superiority persists, reinforced and normalised through societal structure. This includes mechanisms that maintain a hierarchical structure, where whiteness dominates and individuals and groups are measured against their proximity to it (Moreton-Robinson 2000, 2004; hooks 1989; Moses et al. 2004; Goldberg 1993; Herbert 2012[1963]; McGlade 2012). This is a view that aligns with Patricia Hill Collins's (2002) concept of the 'matrix of domination' which outlines how intersecting oppressions are organised. Collins (2002:18) states, 'regardless of the particular intersections involved, structural, disciplinary, hegemonic and interpersonal domains of power reappear across quite different forms of oppressions'. Indigenous women experiencing violence face this continuum of oppression, encountering violence not only from interpersonal relationships but also within service delivery, policy and legislative frameworks.

The concept of intersectionality is informative here. As Kimberlé Crenshaw (2016) argues, 'intersectionality is not primarily about identity. It's about how structures make certain identities the consequences of and the vehicle for vulnerability.' This perspective illuminates the discrimination that Indigenous women encounter at multiple levels and through intersecting axes — such as race, gender, class, sexuality and ableism (Moreton-Robinson 2000; Crenshaw 1991; Collins 2002; hooks 2014). Intersecting forms of oppression reveal how privilege is afforded to certain groups while Indigenous women remain marginalised.

A prevalent misconception is that Indigenous culture is inherently violent — a myth I return to multiple times throughout this book. However, this perspective stems from Western interpretations that misrepresent cultural practices and obscure the Indigenous understanding of conflict resolution and communal relationships (Moreton-Robinson 2000; Crenshaw 1991; Matsuda 2018). These narratives, often left unexamined, are imposed on Indigenous people by Western observers, resulting in profound mischaracterisation of their lived realities. Cognitive dissonance further complicates these dynamics, as it alleviates the discomfort individuals experience when faced with conflicting beliefs and worldviews. Cognitive dissonance can reinforce white supremacy by privileging those who are aligned with the normative values of Australian culture (Lattas 1992).

As Crenshaw (2016) notes, an intersectional framework exposes how the dual positioning of Indigenous women — as both women and members of a subordinated group — affects responses to the violence committed against them. This 'double jeopardy' renders Indigenous women vulnerable to the intersecting dynamics of various forms of oppression. Indigenous women navigate multiple forms of vulnerability engineered by structural institutions, which create distinct challenges.

Indigenous women globally, including Native American, Alaskan and Native Hawaiian women, face unique intersectional discrimination (Anderson 2016; Simpson 2014; TallBear 2019; Trask 1999). Despite maintaining sovereignty over their lands (Anderson 2016; Simpson 2014; TallBear 2019; Trask 1999), they encounter pervasive issues rooted in the dominant force of whiteness. This dynamic translates land appropriation into social capital and wealth for settlers, illustrating a common thread of systemic oppression across different international contexts (Moreton-Robinson 2015).

While Indigenous women across Australia retain a connection to their sovereign land, they contend with vulnerabilities that may intersect with systemic barriers if they seek assistance during a crisis (Matsuda 2018). Many Indigenous women live far from their ancestral lands, due to migration, marriage or historical government removal policies. This separates their experiences from those of other minority or ethnic groups and shows that making assumptions about shared discrimination is overly simplistic (Trask 1999).

Moreover, Indigenous people have been rendered propertyless through the illegal seizure of their land — a reality that is grounded in white possessive logic (Moreton-Robinson 2015). In her critical text,

'Whiteness as property', Cheryl Harris (1993:1715–1718) writes, 'Whiteness defined the legal status of a person as a slave or free ... Whiteness ... is property if by "property" one means all of a person's legal rights.' This highlights that, in Western society, property signifies status and wealth, positioning Indigenous people — especially women — as part of a marginalised population exploited by white settlers, mission managers and government systems (Huggins 1987, 1995; Haskins 2004).

Indigenous women face a unique nexus of intersecting structural vulnerabilities. Their bodies often become commodified under white supremacy, reinforcing the historical context of Indigenous marginalisation within legal and societal frameworks (Moreton-Robinson 2000; Huggins 1987, 1995; Haskins 2004). Understanding these intersectional factors is vital for addressing the systemic violence and discrimination that Indigenous women endure.

VIOLENCE DURING AND SINCE COLONISATION

Before I turn to the stories of the women who share their own experiences of violence in this book, it's important to consider how we have arrived at a position in which violence against Indigenous women in Australia is so widespread. Hence I briefly review violence in Australia since invasion.

Since colonisation, Australia has experienced systemic violence and a carceral framework (that is, a framework that organises social and political life through punishment, surveillance, policing and confinement [Foucault 1979]). The British invasion brought aggressive actions, firearms, foreign substances and new diseases (Maynard 2007; Goodall 2008). As Foucault (1979) describes in his writing about the birth of the prison, Australia manifests as a carceral state, maintaining its colonial legacy through the ongoing containment and institutional control of Indigenous peoples. The penal colony model was built on the idea that those labelled as criminals should be removed from society and confined within controlled spaces. These principles underpinned early colonial governance where the colony utilised confinement as a tool which led to the segregation of Indigenous people onto missions, reserves and reformatories (Baldry et al. 2014). This strategy mirrored broader European colonial practices of controlling populations through coercive and punitive measures rooted in historical practices of public punishment and social intimidation, designed to force conformity.

Throughout the nineteenth and twentieth centuries, these coercive practices evolved but they maintained their core objectives of controlling society and making people conform to British norms. Foucault's (1979:136) concept of docile bodies — that they can be 'subjected, used, transformed, and improved' — is evident in the transformation efforts imposed upon incarcerated people, illustrating how regimes of punishment sought to reshape individual behaviour through surveillance and social conditioning. This approach extended beyond prisons to institutions like schools and hospitals, and reinforced submissive compliance among Indigenous peoples. Despite the process of formal abolition of capital punishment in Australia — as early as 1922 in Queensland and as recently as 1984 in Western Australia (Farrell and O'Sullivan 2025) — the legacy of these oppressive systems is reflected in enduring colonial attitudes and practices that continue to impact Indigenous Australians and their communities.

Australia's colonial methods parallel those imposed in other colonies often using hierarchical structures and enforced Christianisation. Fear-mongering tactics, such as public hangings of Indigenous men, sought to suppress resistance and impose conformity to the British regime. Eighteen years after Captain Cook's invasion, the First Fleet led by Governor Arthur Phillip landed in Kamay (Botany Bay) in 1788 on the lands of the Gadigal people of the Eora Nation (Moreton-Robinson 2015). This arrival introduced diseases such as smallpox, influenza, tuberculosis and sexually transmitted infections that devasted Indigenous communities (Moreton-Robinson 2000; Goodall 2008; Hunter 1993; Organ 1990). It also brought violence through massacres as the colony expanded (Goodall 2008;

Reynolds 2013). As British invaders reached across the country, their preconceived ideas placed Indigenous peoples in an inferior position.

Frontier expansion in Australia led to unprecedented, legalised violence; Bottoms (2013:132) argues the violence was ubiquitous: 'And to justify their behaviour, Europeans portrayed "the blacks" as cannibals and "bad" because they dared to resist the invasion of their homelands and fight a guerilla war'. As settlers pushed further into Indigenous lands, the same racial hierarchy that legalised invasion also shaped the treatment of Indigenous women. On the pastoral frontier, their bodies were folded into the economy of the station as spoken about in ways that stripped them of humanity. Pastoral accounts record, 'Black women were graded: "stud gins" were reserved for the sole use of the boss; class number two were for "colonial experience men" and the third grade were for general hands (Watson 1998:89), a system that treated women as sexual property rather than people.

Watson's (1998) work continues with the violations that extended to Aboriginal children and those born from these encounters. They were ignored in pastoral memoirs unless mentioned as station labour, targeted by Protection Boards or the Native Police, and funnelled into missions and reserves, where separation from family became routine.

During the early colonial era, Indigenous women were routinely dehumanised. They were labelled with derogatory terms such as 'gin' and 'lubra', and colonial narratives cast them as morally deficient and sexually available, positioning them outside the category of respectable womanhood (Robert 2001; Herbert 2012[1963]; Sykes 1975). Although a small number of Indigenous women entered into consensual relationships with white men, historical evidence shows that most interactions occurred in conditions of profound power imbalance and were coercive and non-consensual (Moreton-Robinson 2000; McGrath 1984, 2015; Robert 2001).

A telling illustration of the attitudes that underpinned these practices appears in Xavier Herbert's (2012[1963]:loc. 1056, ebook) autobiographical work *Disturbing element*, where a young boy matter-of-factly repeats what he has learned from adults around him. His comment reveals a worldview in which sexual access to Indigenous women was normalised and trivialised. *'Niggers do it like dawgs, y'know. It don't mean a thing to 'em. So long's you give 'em a bit of a present.'* As with the evidence found in Watson (1998) and Bottoms (2013), these ideas about Indigenous women reflected a wider understanding that Indigenous women were merely stock to be traded for sexual compliance. These undertakings were also sanctioned by Governor Phillip (Tench and Flannery 2009). Today, these practices of sexual exploitation are clearly consistent with human trafficking.

Watkin Tench (2009[1789]), a marine officer of the First Fleet, provides further insight into the early colonial mindset. He noted that vials of smallpox were transported to the colony, writing, 'it is true that our surgeons had brought out variols matter in bottles' (Tench 2009[1789]:104). Although Tench denied any intention of biological warfare, describing such an accusation as 'unworthy of consideration' (2009 [1789]:104), it was well known at the time that smallpox was fatal to populations without prior exposure. Whether deliberate or not, the disease devastated Indigenous communities across the continent, echoing other colonial contexts such as the United States, where infected blankets were distributed to Native American peoples (Mayor 1995). It is possible to suggest that the elimination of Indigenous Australians may have been viewed to facilitate land acquisition and further British colonial expansion (Moses et al. 2004; Kortepeter (ed) 2001). Tench also described a troubling trend that involved procuring Indigenous bodies after death for examination and for shipping overseas to museums and universities (Tench 2009[1789]).

After around 20 years of forced coexistence, relationships between Indigenous peoples and settlers escalated into violence (Moreton-Robinson 2000; Huggins 1995; Goodall 2008; Hunter 1993; Reynolds 1972, 2013; Smithers 2017; Behrendt 1993). White settlers and freed convicts perceived the land as personal property, not as something to be shared and cared for. Moreton-Robinson (2015:xii) describes this as 'white possessive logics', emphasising that ownership of land and resources was claimed by settlers in a way that contrasted with the Indigenous view of themselves as caretakers not owners.

While Aboriginal communities on the mainland faced forced dispossession, displacement and dislocation, Torres Strait Islander communities experienced colonisation differently (Nakata 2007). In the nineteenth and twentieth centuries Islanders were dispossessed of their lands through state and church regulations that imposed Christian morals while simultaneously exploiting marine resources for external markets in a way that benefited non-Islanders rather than the communities themselves (Nakata 2007). The islands were part of a new world with abundant resources ready for white ownership and control (Galtung 1990; Matsuda 2018). As the Torres Strait became commodified, outsiders profited from its natural resources and compelled Islanders to adapt to a new order marked by regulatory control (Nakata 2007). Over time, land and sea resources became profitable possessions claimed by settlers, with Islanders alienated from these profits, along with their ancestral connections (Memmi 2003[1974]).

Indigenous missions and dormitories

In his 1896 work, Archibald Meston observed Indigenous life on the mainland of Queensland. He noted the exploitation of Indigenous women and children, who were often subjected to excessive labour and sexual abuse by white men, and recommended establishing missions to separate Indigenous people from white society to curb these relations (Meston 1896). Each state and territory implemented its own protection policies. In many cases, Indigenous people were forcibly removed from their land. In Queensland this meant that Torres Strait Islanders already living on the mainland became part of the mission structure, while those living in the Torres Strait experienced another form of regimentation and institutionalisation in their home islands. Many children were removed from their families and lived in regimented dormitories, following strict routines and subject to various forms of violence (Wilkie 1997).

Missions and institutions were intended to be protective environments, but they became sites of extreme violence and sexual exploitation for Indigenous women, girls, men and boys. This violence was perpetuated by individuals in authority who implemented state policies and legislation, including government and church agents (Wilkie 1997). Rather than safeguarding and protecting Indigenous children, these authorities imposed colonial control.

White women were complicit in the mission and reserve systems. They often upheld and benefited from these colonial structures and worked as agents of oppression. White women worked as matrons, nurses and teachers, and those who were married supported husbands who had positions of authority. Their complicity highlights the intersection of gender, race and power in enacting oppressive policies against Indigenous people.

Looking at the 'protection' of Indigenous peoples through various colonial systems helps to contextualise the violence that Indigenous women experience today, particularly as missions and reserves mirrored the regimented nature of penal settlements. Run under strict regimes, missions enforced structured activities. Failing to comply often resulted in severe punishment.

The personal testimonies in the *Bringing them home* report about the Stolen Generations illustrate how Indigenous people experienced their institutionalisation as akin to imprisonment (Wilkie 1997). The report includes comments such as, 'I thought I was in a nightmare', 'I couldn't work out what I'd done wrong to deserve this', 'It was like being in prison', 'It was very strict — you weren't allowed to do anything' (Wilkie 1997:133, 144, 137, 138).

Foucault (1979) references Leon Faucher's regimented rules for young prisoners in Paris, emphasising the structured schedule of activities like rising, meals, work and recreation, and highlighting the deprivation of rights and liberty. The model Foucault describes influenced penal practices across Europe and the United States, and thus the approach that evolved in Australia. Like prisons, missions and reserves were positioned on town peripheries, away from society, with the view that those contained within were deviant or criminal.

Coloniser motives and white man's burden

The British Empire was driven by a desire to acquire new lands and resources, which colonisers deemed as a justifiably legal process (Memmi 2003[1974]:52). Ownership of land symbolised wealth and led to the rationalisation of methods used to seize land and marine resources, a mindset that justified settlers' actions without negotiation or regard for Indigenous peoples (Goodall 2008; Reynolds 1972, 2013; Conor 2016; Carlson and Farrelly 2023).

As the colonial project advanced across Australia, it was accompanied by massacres, genocide and ethnocide of Indigenous peoples (Goodall 2008; Reynolds 2013; McGrath 1990; Reynolds 1972). It was supported by a notion that settlers could permanently occupy the land and impose laws brought from their homeland, thereby establishing a new social order in 'settled' regions. This provided a rationalisation for the ongoing violence inflicted on Indigenous peoples, highlighting a troubling legacy of justifying brutality in the pursuit of expansion (Memmi 2003[1974]; Veracini 2010).

The expanding British Empire helped entrench enduring myths about settler identity, casting colonisers as heroic adventurers and righteous pioneers—an ideal portrait that, as Albert Memmi argues, is central to the colonial order (Memmi 2003[1974]:47). These narratives enshrine settlers as heroes in Australian history (Moreton-Robinson 2015, 2022; Carlson and Farrelly 2023) alongside the trope of the 'white man's burden', popularised by Rudyard Kipling's poem first published in McClure's Magazine (Kipling 1899). As poetry and literary culture were highly influential in this period, Kipling's poem is a clear example of the imperial thinking of the time; such ideas provided moral and intellectual cover for frontier brutality (Moreton-Robinson 2015; Harris 1993). Moreton-Robinson further shows how this narrative also recasts settlers as victims of a harsh landscape, thereby disavowing the violence perpetrated against Indigenous people (Moreton-Robinson 2015).

Nakata reinforces this by noting a dualism in narratives that erase Indigenous experiences while framing settlers as impartial heroes, thus perpetuating settler-colonial logic (Nakata 2007). The violence against Indigenous people continued well into the twentieth century and continues today. Entrenched stereotypes depicted Indigenous people as uncivilised and in need of salvation, reinforcing notions of racial inferiority based on faith and culture (Harris 1993; Mills 2003).

Memmi argues the colonial relationship operated as a global system, grounded in shared mechanisms of dispossession, displacement and degradation of Indigenous cultures (Memmi 1965[1957]). In the United States, this structure was embedded in laws that enforced the enslavement and segregation of African Americans, entrenching a political and social order built on white supremacy (Moreton-Robinson 2011; Alexander 2011). This produced a racial hierarchy that pushed Black and Brown people to margins of society under white administrative control, a dynamic reflected across Native American communities and other colonial contexts (Memmi 2003[1974]; Veracini 2010; Harris 1993).

In Australia these same logics further marginalised Indigenous peoples, producing stark disparities in access to rights, resources and recognition. For Indigenous women, this entrenchment of colonial hierarchy was compounded by gender, creating a social stratification in which white women occupied a privilege position solely by virtue of their racial identity (Memmi 2003[1974]; Veracini 2010; Harris 1993). Memmi (2003[1974]:57) succinctly observes, 'the coloniser partakes of an elevated world from which he automatically reaps the privileges'.

Adapting to a foreign and violent culture

The colonisation of Australia initiated severe violence, marked by ongoing frontier wars and retaliatory skirmishes between white settlers and Indigenous peoples. Historian Henry Reynolds classifies this prolonged conflict as a fundamental aspect of Australian history that persisted for up to 140 years (Reynolds 2013:3). Indigenous people faced massacres and violent attacks, with their retaliatory efforts ineffectively matched against the military tactics of white settlers.

Indigenous resistance included highly sophisticated strategies, such as the tactical use of fire to disrupt settler expansion. Pemulwuy, the Bidjigal warrior of the Dharug Nation, led one of the most sustained and organised resistance campaigns with a 12-year revolution against British expansion (Reynolds, 2013:3). Tensions escalated after his death, especially in the Illawarra region of New South Wales, where initial conflicts and abuses by settlers prompted violent retaliations from Indigenous communities. As Michael Organ (1990) notes, these hostilities often arose from settlers' grievances over alleged theft of crops, which Indigenous people viewed as an extension of their traditional rights to land. The settlers' violent reactions, motivated by greed and ignorance, perpetuated cycles of violence and revenge.

This initial phase of colonisation triggered more than immediate conflict: it set in motion a 140-year cycle of frontier violence that Reynolds argues was fundamental to the making of Australia (Reynolds, 2013:3). This continuity of harm produced multigenerational transfer of trauma, where the continued violence of one generation destabilised the next. The prolonged conflict can be seen in events such as the Coniston massacre in 1928 (Reynolds 2013). Indigenous people became aware that coexistence required them to comply with British laws — and that the new laws superseded their own. Under this legal regime, seeking justice was unattainable for Indigenous people because competency to testify required a Christian religious oath, rendering Aboriginal evidence inadmissible unless the witness could satisfy this requirement (Alexander, Nicholls & Plater 2023). They were prohibited from giving evidence in court unless they could demonstrate an understanding of a Christian oath (Skinner 1975). Skinner (1975) explains 'evidence of an Aborigine who did not understand the nature of an oath was inadmissible under the law'.

From an Indigenous viewpoint, colonisation could be seen as punishment for crimes Indigenous people did not commit. Indigenous people likely perceived the ongoing seizure of land as an affront requiring a response and would have viewed their actions as legitimate conflict resolution efforts against encroaching settlers.

Rape as a colonial method of controlling women

In colonial Australia, sexual violence against Indigenous women was not incidental; it was structural. Law, administration and culture worked together to sexualise Indigenous women and to withhold any form of protection when violence occurred. Hannah Robert's work (2001) shows how miscegenation functioned as a biopower (Foucault 1979). Through this process Indigenous women were classified as immoral, which excluded their children and intimate relationships from kinship, rationalised surveillance and justified the removals of mixed-race children (Robert 2001). Thus, experiences of sexual violence and rape were trivialised and minimised when Indigenous women sought the support of colonial institutions for protection. In parallel, Moreton-Robinson (2000) demonstrates white patriarchy and the regulation of Indigenous women's bodies through reproduction and sexuality practices that included sterilisation and the removal of their children. However, a double standard ran through this regime. When Aboriginal women were linked to high-status white men, their sexuality was often romanticised or concealed; some of these men were married and had families of their own with white women (Moreton-Robinson 2000). In contrast, when the men were of a lower socioeconomic status, Indigenous women were labelled prostitutes — ensuring that access to Indigenous women could be tolerated as a vice, but disqualifying them from being family members with the recognition and rights that go with that (Smith 2020). Recent synthesis from the University of Sheffield's *History Matters* also underscores the 'Great Australian Silence' around frontier sexual violence. Smith (2020) notes the connection between colonial and later narratives that rendered assaults on Indigenous women unspeakable in public memory — a pattern that maps onto the under-reporting and discounting of Indigenous women's experiences and what they still face today.

Honouring the life of Mrs Walker

Raping Indigenous women was one way of subjugating them in colonial contexts. It was a method of coercion and control (Moreton-Robinson 2000; McGrath 2015; Robert 2001; Mercer 1975). In Australia, frontier violence included catastrophic genocide. Settlers became masterful at hiding their wrongdoing — including the murder and rape of Indigenous women. Archival records provide details of murders when the victim was a white person, particularly if an Indigenous person was responsible for the death. Much less detail is available recording the rape and murder of Indigenous women. White men's violence against Indigenous women was disregarded and even falsified in coronial records that concealed the actual cause of death.

One example of this comes from the 1880s, where the death of Mrs Mathilda Walker was recorded by Daniel Matthews (1883), a missionary who established the Malgoa Mission in Victoria. Mrs Walker's story has been retold by Nancy Cato (1993[1976]). Mrs Walker died in what was known as Barmah Forest, now Barmah National Park, on the Yorta Yorta lands along the New South Wales and Victoria border. Matthews wrote about an altercation between Mrs Walker's husband and a mob of woodcutters. Mrs Walker's husband was knocked unconscious, and the white men then proceeded to rape Mrs Walker. She was kicked and burned with a piece of hot iron. Due to the extent of her injuries, Mrs Walker passed before police arrived. The three white men were arrested but were acquitted for Mrs Walker's death. Matthews noted that 'the coroner decided they did not have a case to answer' (Cato (1993[1976]:44).

Mrs Walker's murder is one of the earliest written accounts I found in my research documenting both a death and a court proceeding. Her death was tragically common and I know she wasn't the only one. Mrs Walker's story pairs fatal sexual violence with a formal legal proceeding which refused to name the crime. The story demonstrates the denigration of her body and life, and in the coronial report that followed the coroner falsified the cause of death as 'natural causes, accelerated by illness and drink'. Thus, the three white men who were initially charged were exonerated of their wrongdoing as the coroner found there was no case to answer (Robert 2001; Smith 2020). Mrs Walker deserved justice. She also deserved a correct record of the cause of her death.

WHOSE VOICES ARE BELIEVED? WHITE MEDIATION AND INDIGENOUS WOMEN'S CREDIBILITY

The history books do not only show false recordings about causes of death. In my research, I also found records from people who asserted their support of the 'Indigenous cause', but produced contradictory writings that beg the question of whether they were supporting Indigenous issues or merely seeking glorification for being a white person burdened by the harsh reality of living in the Australian outback.

Charles Priest was one such figure. Though treated by some as an ally of the cause, he wrote that rape of Indigenous women was a 'fact of life', minimising its harm to Indigenous women and their families. In 1936 he self-published a pamphlet about the rape of Ms Alice Mindil by a white constable, George Don. At the time of the alleged assault Ms Mindil was working in the Don household for George Don and his wife, Eileen. On what was recorded as her last day of work (13 May 1936), she later reported that George Don assaulted her. Ms Mindil and her de facto husband, Smiler, first reported the assault to police. After inaction by the receiving sergeant, they turned to Priest, who published Alice's sworn declaration. Instead of the allegation being investigated, Priest was later charged with criminal libel (defamation) for publishing her statement. In court at Priest's trial, Ms Mindil, the only prosecution witness, was subjected to cross-examination on her credibility, sexual history and past relationships, while the defence had character testimony from Don's wife, Eileen. Priest distanced himself from the allegations stating:

> [R]aping an Aboriginal woman was common enough fact of life in those days and was not likely to have the traumatic effect on her, or her husband, as it would in the case of a white woman, so why should I dig up such dirt? (Daily Telegraph:5)

There are two issues I want to draw attention to: unreliable witnesses and the pretence of separation.

Unreliable witnesses

The courtroom treatment of Ms Mindil in 1936 — standing alone as the sole Crown witness, subjected to credibility and sexual history cross-examination — makes visible a much older rulebook about who is believable in Australian courts. Long before Ms Mindil entered a Darwin courtroom, Reverend Lancelot Threlkeld was speaking of a system that would refuse to hear Indigenous people's testimony. He condemned the system by stating it was 'mere legal fiction' while still declaring 'Christian laws will hang the Aborigines… but will not protect them' because they could not testify under a Christian oath (Threlkeld:1841:2). Threlkeld's writings in annual and public reports in the late 1830s–1840s expose the contradiction with unusual clarity.

The case record shows how this disbelief was legally manufactured. In *R v Jackey* (1834), defence counsel protested that Aboriginal witnesses could not be called at all — they were deemed 'incompetent' oath takers (Alexander, Nicholls and Plater 2023). In *R v Dundomah* (1840), the NSW Attorney General openly acknowledged the 'great disadvantage' to Aboriginal defendants whose tribal witnesses were excluded (Alexander, Nicholls and Plater 2023). And in the Myall Creek prosecutions (1838–1839), proceedings were adjourned for months to 'instruct' an Aboriginal eyewitness in the nature of an oath; the Attorney General ultimately conceded there was no realistic chance of making him 'competent', and the case fell away (Alexander, Nicholls and Plater 2023). Each step signals a structural, not individual, credibility problem.

As the New South Wales timeline notes, this oath barrier amounted to a 'denial of justice' until late reforms admitted unsworn testimony from Indigenous people — yet even then courts and juries were taught to discount its weight against sworn evidence from non-Indigenous witnesses (Alexander, Nicholls and Plater 2023). Those learned hierarchies of belief did not vanish; they echo forward into twentieth-century proceedings. These ideas persisted in 1936, explaining why Ms Mindil's evidence was vulnerable to discounting while white reputational claims were privileged, culminating not in an assault prosecution but in Priest's criminal libel conviction, and no justice for Ms Mindil.

Pretence of separation

Building from Ms Mindil's court experience, colonial print culture and legal practice produced what Hannah Robert (2001) terms the 'pretence of separation'. Indigenous women were cast as a different, and lesser, womanhood — hypersexualised, immoral and, therefore, non-credible — while 'purity' and protection were reserved for white women. The framing naturalised violence against Indigenous women and pre-sorted credibility against them, even when they did speak (Robert 2001). In Ms Mindil's 1936 case, we see the pretence at work: white reputational evidence, the constable's 'good character' and his wife's testimony were foregrounded. Meanwhile, Ms Mindil was cross-examined through credibility and sexual-history attack lines, a courtroom script consistent with the longer nineteenth-century pattern of first excluding Aboriginal voices under oath and later discounting their weight once admitted (Alexander, Nicholls and Plater 2023; Daily Telegraph 1936; Truth 1936; Towards Truth n.d.). Contemporary scholarship shows how these colonial sexual narratives have persisted in shaping perceptions of Indigenous women's sexuality and believability, reinforcing the non-ideal victim trope unless actively countered in law and practice (Robert 2001; Sullivan 2018).

THE 'IDEAL VICTIM' AND HOW BLAME IS REASSIGNED TO VICTIM SURVIVORS

The criminal legal system still operates with a tacit template of the 'ideal victim' — a figure who most readily gains full and legitimate victim status (Christie 1986). In Nils Christie's account, that person is weak relative to the offender, blameless, attacked while engaged in a respectable activity, and distanced from any conduct that could invite doubt (Christie 1986: 17–30). The more a complainant deviates from those attributes, the more credibility work they must do to be believed. For Indigenous women, this is a near-structural disqualification: the colonial pretence of separation has long coded them outside respectability and purity, making the harm they experience appear ordinary and their testimony suspect (Robert 2001).

In practice, 'ideal victim' markers are policed both informally and formally, through these ways as described by Christie. These ideal victim markers operate through false equivalence: they are treated as universal and neutral criteria, even though they assume all women can or should present in ways shaped by white, middle-class femininity.

- **Innocent and blameless:** Defence strategy and courtroom commonsense often invert this to ask what the complainant did wrong — for example, prior relationships with the accused, late reporting, combative or non-compliant, or giving 'mixed messages'. These are classic non-ideal cues in Christie's framework and have predictable effects on assessments of credibility.

- **Respectable and conforming:** Where a complainant's life is read as 'chaotic' (poverty, prior criminalisation, prior experience of violence or being considered the aggressor), fact-finders can import stereotypes that discount reliability.
- **Emotionally distraught and uncooperative:** Flat affect, delayed disclosure or reluctance to retell the story are read against the ideal script. Even though trauma research and cross-cultural linguistics would predict variability in how complainants present, Indigenous witnesses may be misread through features such as gratuitous concurrence.
- **No deviance, no history:** Any prior offending, substance use or contact with child protection feeds into doubt that maps directly onto the non-ideal label and narrows perceived prospects of conviction.

CONNECTING THE PAST AND THE PRESENT

Australia's colonial history echoes the violence experienced today by Indigenous women. Historically, white male patriarchy was the mechanism used to claim possession of Indigenous lands and Indigenous people (Moreton-Robinson 2000; Deer 2015; Linklater 2014; Smith 1999). That history connects to the present through the cumulative effects of intergenerational trauma (Deer 2015; Linklater 2014; Atkinson 2002), an unresolved grief described in Native American communities as 'soul wounds' (Duran et al. 1998). The transmission of intergenerational trauma happens when children adapt and adopt behaviours and beliefs that served a purpose at some point in history as a mechanism of survival (DeGruy 2005).

Today, Indigenous women experience violence at both interpersonal and structural levels. Interpersonal violence can be episodic or cyclical, one-off or repetitive. Interpersonal violence doesn't fit neatly into any descriptive box and is best viewed along a continuum that intersects the various environments in which Indigenous women live and interact. At the structural level, we need to consider both the social systems that can impose violence, and the systems and structures through which Indigenous women may seek support. In Aboriginal and Torres Strait Islander communities, there are communities within communities within communities, with intersecting domains that require specialised understanding. Any of these communities can be points of discrimination where further violence happens.

Many Indigenous communities are close-knit, with a web of family connections involving both blood and non-blood relations. These connections require an agile service system that recognises, acknowledges and honours relationships. Service providers need to understand how family and community connections can either facilitate or impede service delivery.

Contextualising aggression: provocation and retaliation

Indigenous communities have long been unfairly perceived as violent, with the perception of violence rooted in narratives constructed by early settlers and white anthropologists (Moreton-Robinson 2000; Hiatt 1996; Kaberry 2004). Early writers crafted an ideology of 'savagery and treachery', and, as Hunter (1993:13) further notes, 'explorers and settlers anticipated and often provoked intercultural conflict', reinforcing their preconceived notions of Indigenous peoples as primitive. Such biased observations laid the groundwork for viewing Indigenous cultures as barbaric and violent.

Dwyer and Nettelbeck (2018:10) point out that many disciplines 'failed to historically contextualise violence'. The perception that Indigenous communities are inherently violent began with European notions, with Indigenous people classified as uncivilised savages (Hiatt 1996). French anthropologist Paul Broca (1867:46) asserted that 'never has a people with black skin ... spontaneously arrived at colonisation'. These views failed to recognise the sophisticated legal systems and social structures that governed Indigenous communities prior to colonisation, including adherence to tribal boundaries and the resolution of grievances through culturally sanctioned means (Williams 1987).

The clash between Indigenous and European worldviews led to cycles of provocation and retaliation. Europeans frequently misinterpreted Indigenous conflict resolution as warfare, leading to violent actions involving artillery and eventually, in Australia, the inclusion of the Native Police in efforts to suppress Indigenous resistance (Hunter 1993; Reynolds 2013; Langton 1988; Organ 2014; Williams 1987; Burbank 1994). In 1955, anthropologist Les Hiatt emphasised that early European observers did not understand Indigenous governance and intercommunity relations, which were governed by strict customary law (Williams 1987). For example, grievances among Yolŋu people often centred around violations of resource rights, ceremonial processes and breaches of communal obligations (Williams 1987).

Misconceptions persisted as early male observers portrayed their interactions with Indigenous people through a distorted lens, emphasising violence based on hearsay rather than direct observations (Tonkinson and Burbank 2017). For instance, depictions of marriage through theft failed to consider the communal system that included cultural practices, and those practices surrounding mourning and other expressions of grief.

Early reports in 1814 by Lachlan Macquarie, Governor of New South Wales, documented violence against Indigenous women by settlers and reflected the provocation that led to Indigenous retaliation (Organ 1990, 2014; Langton 1988). During the punitive expeditions of 1816, Macquarie's approach turned towards violence and oppression when he instructed military forces to treat Indigenous people as prisoners of war and instil terror through public executions and by the hanging of Indigenous men 'in conspicuous locations' (Organ 2014:4). Fundamentally, this was a warning to the Indigenous community of the consequences of non-compliance.

Conflict resolution and adaptation to violence

Indigenous dispute resolution centred on the violation of communal laws often linked to personal relationships rather than land issues (Hunter 1993; Reynolds 2004, 2013; Langton 1988; Burbank 1994). Such processes were rooted in egalitarian principles, contrasting sharply with colonial power structures that imposed British laws and classified Indigenous people as possessions of the state. This misunderstanding of Indigenous practices and governance ultimately obscured the rich social fabric of egalitarianism that existed prior to colonisation.

The colonial white lens remarked on the 'excitable temperament' that could lead to squabbles among Indigenous peoples (Haddon, in Nakata 2007:127). What must be acknowledged, as Hiatt (1996:84) observed, is that 'inter-tribal battles were conducted with formality, in accordance with agreed principles and an established code of honour'. Unlike the violent retribution often associated with contemporary conflict, these systems aligned with Indigenous communal governance processes that sought to ensure community harmony and understanding.

The violence imposed by colonisers continues to affect communities today. Present-day violence, which often results in severe injuries, differs significantly from the conflict resolution methods embedded in Indigenous cultural law and redressive action. Historical and anthropological evidence attributes this shift towards violence to the disruption of cultural practices and the influence of white male patriarchy. In short, some Indigenous people have adopted methods of Western violence.

For Indigenous people, the result is a type of lateral violence, or horizontal oppression, that incites unrest and conflict through adverse interactions between community members. It manifests at individual, cultural and structural levels and results in violence as a typical response — including legitimate acts of resistance and self-defence, often enacted by women who try to protect themselves and their children.

Over time, Indigenous people's perceptions of violence have evolved, as described in Foucault's (1979) work on punishment and discipline. What was once considered violent is different from how we currently interpret it, and it differs in Western and Indigenous contexts. Adopting Western cultural norms for survival has led to a widespread misinterpretation of violence as being inherent to Indigenous culture. Violence has been internalised and erroneously embodied in Indigenous communities. It manifests in various forms — physical, psychosocial, mental, emotional and spiritual.

There is a crucial distinction between aggression, conflict resolution and violence — a differentiation often misunderstood by non-Indigenous observers. Aggression typically arises when emotions are expressed in a way that is perceived as hostile. Conflict resolution, a vital aspect of Indigenous redressive action, is frequently misinterpreted as violence. True violence however, manifests directly against individuals or groups through interpersonal, communal, systemic or structural means. It encompasses emotional, financial, mental, physical, spiritual and sexual, and verbal and written communication. Violence is about power, and exerting it can have profound, long-term impacts on people and their communities.

The multigenerational impact of trauma experienced by Indigenous people has encouraged adaptation to Western violence and cultural norms. The infrastructure of violence has evolved from being an open spectacle, such as the public display of violence at public executions, to more insidious forms, such as surveillance and removal. For Indigenous peoples survival necessitated assimilation, which often required them to become Christianised and adopt Western values. At times, assimilation (which can be seen as coercive submission) was resisted by Indigenous communities. However, colonial policies mandated conformity and imposed severe consequences on those who resisted.

Today, the historical framing of Indigenous communities as savage or barbaric remains entrenched in the ways Indigenous people are perceived and reinforces harmful stereotypes about Indigenous people as violent. I believe that violence in Indigenous communities is often misunderstood and judged without considering the broader context of cumulative trauma, cultural law, conflict resolution and systemic issues.

As this book shows, violence towards Indigenous women and children has become endemic and has been commandeered by ill-informed writers of history. I must also acknowledge that some Indigenous men have adopted and adapted to white male patriarchal violence and now believe it is their right to own and control Indigenous women. This type of violence does not belong in Indigenous communities and violence against women is not an accepted Indigenous practice. Any claims that it is part of Indigenous cultural custom reflects a misuse of cultural practices and the adaptation of white male patriarchal violence. Violence against Indigenous women should never be confused with the cultural processes of conflict resolution.

PART B

Shattering the Silence

CHAPTER 3

WE REFUSE TO BE SILENCED: STORIES OF SURVIVAL

> There's a saying that I have: Through struggle there's strength. The outcome of ... the struggle and the strength that you gain from the struggle, is getting through hard experiences. (**Jaylah**)

In this chapter, and in the following chapters in this part, the women I interviewed speak directly to you. Along the way, I provide an insight into the violence they experienced, the coping mechanisms they developed, the sense of safety they found in some places and their ongoing injuries.

CHALLENGING THE ERASURE OF INDIGENOUS WOMEN

Indigenous women in Australia face numerous stereotypes and discriminatory practices that stem from white ideology and imposed inscriptions, stereotypes that frequently emerge from misconceptions about Indigenous identity and culture. Nia illustrates this by discussing her experiences with people who make assumptions about her racial background, leading them to express stereotypical views based on a false assumption.

> Sometimes people assume that I'm from a Pacific Islander background. They don't know I'm Indigenous so sometimes they'll just start bringing up racist or culturally inappropriate stuff thinking that

> I'm not Indigenous [and thinking] I'm not going to be offended. People that know me, know I'm black, but some people who I've not crossed, just think I'm Māori, or I'm Pacific Islander so they just make assumptions. (**Nia**)

The erasure and mischaracterisation of Indigenous women persists in society and often fits them into a particular mould. Jaylah describes her typical response:

> I really don't give a shit what people think about me, they can call me angry all they want. I'm assertive, I know where I want to be in the world and if you can't handle me I don't give a fuck. (**Jaylah**)

Jaylah's resistance to stereotypes highlights her agency and self-definition, and illustrates how Indigenous women move beyond imposed and limited constructs.

Indigenous women are objectified, often in a way that involves hypersexualisation — both historically and through current media narratives. Terms like 'black velvet,' which refer to the sexual exploitation of Indigenous women by white men, underscore the media's role in perpetuating these harmful stereotypes (Moreton-Robinson 2000; McGrath 1984, 1990; Conor 2016). Jaylah contextualises this within the legacy of colonisation:

> It's one of those things about Indigenous women being the sex objects. Indigenous women being sexualised and this idea around the exotic other. So if you're not submissive, it comes back to the way ... Australia has been colonised and how Indigenous women have been used as sex objects. (**Jaylah**)

Racism is deeply entrenched within Australian norms and policies. Indigenous women describe pervasive encounters with racism and discrimination that span generations (Delgado and Stefancic 2017; Ladson-Billings and Tate 1995; Nadal 2018; Solorzano et al. 2000). Jaylah elaborates on this, pointing to systemic structures that perpetuate oppression.

> My issue is we get so caught up talking about the individual experiences of violence, and rightly so, and getting individual women into safe places and out of crisis situations. What we don't talk about is the racism, is the racist policies, the oppressive and structures like when you start talking about systems that are designed to separate families, like the child protection system. When you start talking about legislation, that's designed — and organisations like state government, like the court systems — [they're] designed to protect the perpetrator. And if you're an Indigenous woman socially constructed in a specific way ... then you've got this thing of, 'oh, it's only [a] black thing'. Well, no, it's not, it's a societal thing and it's structural and it's systemic. (**Jaylah**)

Jaylah referred to the case of Ms Dhu, who died in custodial care (Coroner's Court of Western Australia 2016). Ms Dhu's story exemplifies how racial stereotypes and systemic failures contribute to Indigenous women's marginalisation.

> Those discriminations that happen on those levels, like, say for instance, the stuff that happened with Ms Dhu and her dying in custodial care. Those white people that didn't look after her, there was a lack of duty of care because of their belief of who she was as an Indigenous woman. So it comes down to the individual level the way in which you've been raised, how you perceive Indigenous people to be. Then it's the systems and the policies and the legislations and the structures that silence us and erase us and our voices. (**Jaylah**)

Jaylah highlights the systemic issues that need to be urgently addressed. They extend beyond individual prejudices to the broader structures that silence and erase Indigenous voices.

Globally, there is a rising resistance against white supremacy — both among Indigenous populations and in the African diaspora. Jaylah discusses this in the global context, noting that all Indigenous and non-white peoples are categorised based on their proximity to whiteness.

> In this period, what I'm seeing, not just here in Australia but on a global scale, this resurgence or this pushback by Indigenous people, by Indigenous peoples across the world, people within the African diaspora, including African Americans. And it's all against white supremacy and whiteness. People must understand that this is the world that we live in. We are judged, we are created, we are spoken about in terms of our relationship to whiteness and to white supremacy. And that's why I'll always argue the case that as an Indigenous woman, race comes first and foremost. (**Jaylah**)

DESCRIBING VIOLENCE

> The worst thing I ever went through was my son telling me it was time to leave and I was black and blue, the blood was everywhere. The blood was all through the sheets, my face was split up and I had broken ribs. I could hardly walk and breathe. He laid his head on my shoulder and looked me fair smack in the eyes with an icepack in his hand, and said, 'it's time to leave because next time dad punches or hits you he's going to kill you and I don't want that', and he cried. For a six-year-old, nearly seven, to do that is life changing. The violence was one thing but when it started to affect my son in that way, the decision was made. I explained to him there and then, if I left I wasn't coming back, there's no way I'd go back. His reply was — well, let's go. (**Jemila**)

When we spoke, the women and families described their experiences of violence with hindsight, and the violence was clearly visible. However, in the moments when violence occurs, the power and control can sometimes be masked by the perpetrator and thus hidden — sometimes even from the woman herself. One common theme from all the women I interviewed was that violence related to control. Their experiences of violence varied, but the perpetrator took and kept power in their relationship.

The women and families described many types of violence, including experiences related to coercive control, psychological violence, financial violence, physical violence, sexual violence, rape, stalking, isolation, power and control, abduction and being held hostage. The family members of those who had been murdered described witnessing these forms of violence in their loved ones' relationships. The perpetrators also varied — the perpetrator could be a partner, family member or friend. Some of the women had witnessed violence as children, teenagers or adults.

The women collectively understood that violence is complex and nuanced — it's different for everyone.

> I'm aware that it's quite complicated. It's power [and] control over someone whether that's physical, sexual. That violence of someone standing over someone and really intimidating. (**Jemila**)

The definition of violence varies, depending on who is involved. Each woman had her own way of understanding and describing it. For example, Kya shared a distinction between domestic and family violence:

> Domestic violence for me is with your partner, yeah, like with your intimate partner, whereas family violence might be with your cousin or your brother/sister or whatever, something like that. (**Kya**)

Psychological violence and the early stages of a relationship

Many of the women described the early stages of a relationship as a process of grooming, where the person who used violence tested the boundaries by applying various forms of psychological violence, including coercion. As the relationship continued, sometimes other types of violence, such as financial and verbal abuse, also started. In time, many relationships involved physical and sexual violence, which often started when the women resisted the perpetrators' demands.

> He used to put me down a lot. I was either too skinny or I was too fat or everything that I sort of did was wrong but then everything I did was right, you know, and then everything I did was wrong, it was just this cycle, it just went on and on. (**Malia**)

Nia described the violence as a process that occurred gradually. It was something she didn't particularly notice, but can now understand.

> The physical violence didn't start until I fell pregnant with my first child, and we were together for 12 months, but the power struggle and the power violence and verbal crap was already there, it was already instilled and because it was a gradual thing, I didn't really notice it. (**Nia**)

The gradual progression of violence involves the perpetrator using violence to isolate, and obtain power and control.

> At about six months in [to the relationship] he showed jealous streaks, just by some of the things he would say to me. Then he accused me of chatting up to some guy when we were out at a club. Three months later he gave me the hiding of my life ... That first beating was the worst, and I was scared from then. From there on, there were certain

> things that I'd do and say, but would stop at a certain point. Then I'd just have to shut up. Or I'd get slapped, backhanded or whatever else he'd want to sling at me. (**Jaylah**)

Jaylah's account of the severity of her first experience of physical assault reflects a process identified by Michael P Johnson (2008: 49), whereby women experiencing violence for the first time often interpret it as a one-off event rather than as part of an ongoing pattern of abuse. As Johnson notes, while such violence may initially be understood as anomalous, in cases of 'intimate terrorism' women may slowly come to recognise that they are confronting a stable pattern of power and control.

Without an understanding of coercive control, intimidation and the perpetrator's pattern of violence, Jaylah may have initially thought she was experiencing situational violence — that is, a one-off incident. In time, she understood the pattern, but her first experience of violence remained her benchmark.

> It's kind of like that trade-off; this time it's only a backhand, it wasn't a full-on beating, you know. When I talk about my first beating being the worst, well, it was. I ended up with a black eye, busted eye vessels ... You know, when your blood vessels in your eye burst from being hit, grazed hands and knees from where I fell down on the cement, lumps on the back of my head as he grabbed hold of my head and hit it against the wall near where I fell. He beat me bad. So that was kind of like the benchmark. Anything not as extreme as that, wasn't that bad. (**Jaylah**)

While Jaylah's initial experience provided her benchmark, over time she started to feel that psychological abuse created a longer-term problem.

> So you put up with the verbal abuse, but after a while, it's that saying when someone tells you something for so long you tend to believe it, the psychological abuse is really ... it's the worst. I can deal with [a] bruise, but it's the mental stuff that goes on years later. (**Jaylah**)

Calculated violence

Most of the violence we discussed happened in the home, but sometimes it occurred in public places. Most physical and sexual violence occurred in the bedroom, but not exclusively. Jemila described a journey through the house, which finished in the bedroom.

> We'd go down the hallway and I'd just walk nice and timely down to the [bedroom] ... he'd turn every TV on between where our children were playing and our room. That's where I took it, and I took a lot, and I couldn't yell out because if I did the kids would come to the door. (**Jemila**)

Several of the women talked about physical violence, and in some cases it occurred almost as soon as the relationship started. In other relationships, physical and sexual violence occurred after a period of less visible violence, including coercive control and psychological violence.

Some of the women described assaults that resulted in bruising, but in locations where bruises could be hidden.

> He would never hit me in a place where a bruise could be seen on my face. And because I've got long hair, I guess he worked out that hitting me on the side of the face with his palms or forearms or an open palm was better than a closed fist, bruises could be hidden. When I ducked down and held my hands up just to cover my face, he was able to hit me on the side of the head like around the temple on both sides.

> So, I had bruises and I was really sore on the side of my face that would be covered by my hair. (**Jaylah**)

Jaylah experienced physical violence that was done carefully — it was calculated to hide bruises while still inflicting pain. Keeping the violence hidden or changing the method does not discount the harm the women experienced.

> On the body, he would try and choke me, he only choked me when it was wintertime, believe that or not, because I used to wear a lot of scarves and could cover it. He was a very meticulously, well planned out man. (**Keira**)

The violence Keira described was non-fatal strangulation. Sometimes, strangulation is performed as part of sexual activities and in some relationships it may be considered normal. But non-fatal strangulation is a crime, and the activity is dangerous. In all Australian states and territories, specific legislation now identifies intentional strangulation as a standalone offence. In 2018 New South Wales was the first state to amend its *Crimes Act 1900* this way. Victoria introduced changes in 2023 and 2024. Like Keira, Darrabarra described being choked:

> I'm only just starting to deal with this with my own counsellor, and he noticed a few things that I was doing, and he said, 'I notice you touch your neck a lot', and I said, 'Yeah, I hated it … he — because he tried to choke me, you know?' (**Darrabarra**)

In some cases, violence was compounded by substance use. In some examples the perpetrator had various addictions and used violence to obtain money. Standing over someone involves being domineering and demanding (Barnett et al. 2010). Lani described an experience:

> I would get a little bit of money from Centrelink and he would stand over that. If I didn't give him money to go and score [get drugs], he would crack up and go into horrors, so there's a lot of that control and standing over and I was very fearful of him, very fearful, and scared for my kids because he was unpredictable in that state of mind, where he's on drugs and don't care. (**Lani**)

Several of the women had been married to the people who used violence. When they approached the topic of divorce, it was used as another method of control, with their partners controlling them by refusing to sign the divorce papers or attempting to reconcile.

> We didn't get divorced for about four or five years because he kept refusing to sign the papers, and even the day before we were going to the court to have it all done, he phoned me ... I had it on speaker for like an hour and he was, like, you can't do this to me. We'd been separated for six years ... He had moved on several times [laugh] and done the same thing. (**Kima**)

Sexual violence

Several women discussed sexual violence, including rape and coercion to participate in sexual activities. To better understand the difference between rape and sexual assault, while terms may differ across jurisdictions I adopt the following national definitions when referring to rape and sexual assault separately.

> Rape — the Australian Law Reform Commission defines rape as: 'the penetrative sexual offence... generally includes penetration of the genitalia by a penis, object, part of a body or mouth... without the consent of the complainant' (ALRC 2010:[25.8]–[25.12]).

> Sexual assault — Australia's *National Plan to End Violence against Women and Children 2022–2032* describes sexual assault as sexual activity without free and voluntary consent, including forced, coerced or manipulated sexual activity, covering sexualised touching, sexual abuse, sexual assault and rape (AIHW 2025:2).

Several of the women I spoke to experienced sexual violence and rape. Some followed through with legal proceedings, while others did not. Their reasons for reporting (or not) also differed. Sexual violence can be a form of denigration and a tool of power performed for the perpetrator's self-gratification.

> He had a high sex drive, and I wasn't like that, so I don't even know how we lasted that long. I remember we were up in the room, and I think I just had given birth to my eldest son, I went upstairs, I had a shower and then I got out of the shower. He came in the room and closed the door and basically had his way with me. Not long after, my daughter walks in, you know, and it was, like, I can't even look at her. **(Darrabarra)**

Several women said they were coerced and forced to participate in sexual acts, including being forced to have sex with other people. Some described this as rape, while others described the perpetrator as 'taking' sex from them. In many cases, the perpetrators were already violent, so the women knew that further violence was likely if they did not comply.

> He raped me and that's how, you know, [my child] was conceived, and then I never, ever thought about it [until]... I started talking to my counsellor, because the DV [domestic violence] there was really bad. **(Darrabarra)**

When he abducted me, he actually raped me. I suffered from his hand and was drugged and raped by him and someone else whom I [am] still unsure of, I only remember the lighter being flicked and then it's all blurred. I was drugged because I lost time when I was waking, I remember laying on my tummy with my hands tied behind my head. (**Aiyana**)

The sexual abuse on top of the DV was almost like just the straw that broke the camel's back sort of thing and I ended up pregnant again to that man and now having two little children. I didn't have any family or support and, I don't know, it was the most terrifying, most traumatic thing I've ever been through and I think as a society, that's sad because motherhood should be the most beautiful thing that can happen to you and having children and creating a family should be the most beautiful natural thing to do. (**Kima**)

When I first came out and said something to my mum about this guy, when I was nine years old, [she said,] 'Don't be stupid', da-da-da. But back then everything used to be hush-hush, everything gets swept under the carpet. And so that was it. And then it happened again a few times, and I just can't tell anyone. If my mum didn't believe me, who's going to believe me? (**Keira**)

Between the floggings or the beatings or whatever, but when [my daughter] was born it sort of stopped for about six weeks, I think the longest break was six weeks. Then he became a very, very abusive man, as in sex. He took it. When he wanted. I ended up pregnant at my six-week check-up after having an emergency caesarean. (**Keira**)

The stuff with him, with the violence, it got worse after he had been in prison. That's when the sex got rougher as well. (**Jaylah**)

> You couldn't say no to sex, you were kicked out of bed because 'that's my bed', like he owned everything, he owned me, he owned my child, you know, I didn't even have a purse, I'd never paid a bill. **(Akira)**

Several of the women were pregnant when the violence occurred, and were concerned about the health of their unborn child. For Aiyana, violence led to her being hospitalised periodically during her pregnancy. One time when Aiyana attended the hospital, the police were there and spoke to her. However, she could not speak to them in private because the perpetrator was with her. He controlled the situation and he controlled what the police were told. To keep Aiyana and the baby safe, the hospital staff and the police should have ensured her partner was not present during the consultation.

> Throughout my pregnancy I was constantly at the hospital because I was in and out of labour from about 20 weeks ... He would kick me in the stomach, punch me ... When I was very newly pregnant, like, only not long found out, he'd run me over with a car, like it was slow, but hurt my knee ... We used to live in flats so someone called the ambulance and the police came to the hospital but he was there. My daughter was born eight weeks prematurely because of the violence, she's got some issues now because of the trauma that was received during the pregnancy. **(Aiyana)**

Ongoing injuries and psychological impacts

In our conversations, the women talked about broken jaws, broken ribs, other broken bones, fractured skulls, head injuries, hip and back injuries, teeth dislodgement, lacerations that required suturing because of knife wounds, superficial wounds, bruising, black eyes and spontaneous labour while pregnant. Many of the women were still experiencing the impact and ongoing health implications of violence when we spoke.

> I suffered head injuries, hip injuries, back injuries, as well as multiple other superficial injuries that healed but I live with the back, the hip, the head [injuries] every day. (**Nia**)

> I guess my most serious injury was the last assault that he actually did get charged for and the violence order that stayed in place and then it expired, he actually knocked my two front teeth, he punched me in the mouth, so I wear a partial plate up at the top. (**Djinda**)

Some women sustained disabilities with long-term complications like an inability to work or reduced cognitive function. Several reported ongoing health issues that resulted from their injuries, including back and neck conditions and ongoing mental health concerns. These issues continued to affect the women daily, even years after leaving the violent relationship. In some cases, they affected the women's ability to secure employment. Ongoing health issues limited Kima's ability to find work and restricted the jobs she felt she could manage.

> I was on Centrelink [payments] and I was in the disability trust trying to get employment, I've been a single parent ... because I have the mental illness. [Post-traumatic stress disorder] is a major issue, I'm claustrophobic, I get restless, I have anxiety, I have depression, I can only do certain jobs. Like gardening. (**Kima**)

The psychological impacts of violence manifest in different ways for different women. Many women mentioned conditions such as post-traumatic stress disorder, anxiety and depression. For Jaylah the long-term psychological impacts remain.

> The emotional and psychological damage: I was diagnosed with [post-traumatic stress disorder] and high-functioning anxiety, which is weird to me. But at the same time, I can see why I am high functioning. When I was in that relationship what I could control was food that went in my mouth, my education and work, so that's what I did. I'm fortunate in a way, that ... I've become quite qualified in terms of my education. I've done a degree and postgraduate studies and have a successful career, but I hid this violence at the same time ... I think I could deal with the beatings because the bruise goes away but it was the psychological stuff that I struggle with even today. (**Jaylah**)

Seeking medical help

Some of the women described a conscious choice to either seek or not seek medical help. Pregnant women experiencing violence may be more likely to be admitted to hospital, while non-pregnant women may self-assess to decide whether their injuries are serious enough to warrant medical attention. In some cases, though, medical attention is unavoidable. For example, Kya was escorted to hospital because of injuries sustained when she was beaten with a piece of wood. Neighbours called the ambulance, but her cousin helped her get to hospital.

> I was walking [away], I got to the end of fence line, [and] the next minute he came across the road and he had a big bit of wood in his hand. I woke up on the ground in a foetal position and I didn't realise I was hurt. My cousin came and picked me up; I passed out. [I was taken to hospital by my cousin.] She [my cousin] said she'd never seen it before, but [at hospital] there was a wheelchair sitting there, [I was still unconscious and] she just lifted me out of the car, put me in the wheelchair, rolled me in and I never came to [consciousness] until,

> I don't know what time it was, but all I heard them saying was they've got to cut my hair to get to all of the cuts in my head. I ended up with five staples at the front just near my temple, seven staples up the back and lacerations. I couldn't see out of one eye, and then the next day both eyes were closed. (**Kya**)

While Kya had no choice about hospitalisation, Anika self-assessed to decide whether her injuries were serious enough to warrant a hospital visit. What isn't said in Anika's comment is how someone decides whether an injury is severe enough for hospitalisation — though perhaps the suggestion of an ambulance is an indication.

> Well, because you just wouldn't [call the ambulance] because I think back then, a punch around the head or a black eye or whatever, was not an ambulance-calling offence, if you know what I mean. You just ... that's kind of, like, you got a punch in the head and you might have had a bit of a blackout or whatever, but it wasn't like, oh, let's ring the ambulance, you might have concussion or whatever. (**Anika**)

Anika said the hospital felt like an unsafe place, where she was treated differently from others — though she didn't say how or why.

> I don't think the hospital would have been a safe place back then. No, you would have been treated differently. (**Anika**)

It's possible that Anika was referring to previous discrimination, and she mentioned 'being judged in many ways'. For Kima, being hospitalised provided a break from the violence and her partner. She saw hospital as a respite and a safer place than home.

> I'd always wind up in hospital, but I liked being in hospital, [it] was good for me because I had a rest and I was safe in hospital. (**Kima**)

To leave her violent relationship, Anika pretended to take an overdose of medication while pregnant. By attending the hospital with an overdose, she was able to seek support from health staff. The hospital staff contacted the police, who escorted her out of the town so she could return to her home community.

> I pretended to take an overdose. I had a bit of nursing background, I knew if they made you vomit, I wanted to have some tablets there so they could say I've taken something, so I took that and something else. I don't know what it was, but it was just enough. The ambulance took me to the hospital. When I was in the hospital, they gave me the medicine and I'm vomiting and whatever and I had a threatened miscarriage, the doctor and the social worker came. I just said to them, well, this is what's happening, I am trapped here. I'm five-and-a-half months pregnant, I've been bashed around since I got with this person. I don't want to be there. So, they called the police, which was good. They [the police] went around [to the house] and got my stuff and they took me to the train station. I got on the train and left, I never ever went back to that person. (**Anika**)

When Jemila described her injuries, she said that she did not seek medical attention even though she knew her ribs were broken.

> They [my ribs] were broken, I'll tell you, they were ... Took me months but by the time I healed, it was back again and the timeframes between hidings got shorter and shorter. (**Jemila**)

The perpetrator's patterns

Most of the women understood the signs of imminent violence and would subconsciously but methodically prepare for what was to come. Most said they could sense where the situation was heading and patterns of violence that were likely to occur. Keira described the perpetrator as 'meticulous' and 'controlled'.

> No one picked it up. I was really good at [hiding] it. I became expert, like I could have broken ribs and bruises like you've never seen all over my body and it could be hidden and it was with clothes that I used to wear to work ... So you could see the sunburn marks to here so he knew what he was doing. It wasn't a fit of rage, it was meticulous. (**Keira**)

Malia described how the perpetrator controlled her and restricted her access to family.

> He was just manipulative, because I hadn't had very much contact with my family; I had, like, no friends by that stage. I said to him one time, I'm going to go to my mum and dad, and he used it against me, he got my mum to come over to our house and he basically made my mum think that I was crazy or something, like he put it on. (**Malia**)

For Keira, the violence extended beyond physical abuse to include financial abuse, verbal abuse, intimidation and manipulation. The perpetrator sought power and control. However, Keira was the main income earner in the relationship, and her perpetrator depended on her for resources and money.

> He had the physical violence, which you heal from. He was good at manipulation and mental games. He was good at the verbal abuse

> and the abuse of power. He didn't work, I worked, I bought the house, but the keycard would always be gone and [money] would always be spent and it progressively got worse. (**Keira**)

Several women described the stories they invented to hide the violence and explain their injuries.

> I said I was jumping a fence because he'd actually sliced my throat, so, yeah, I said I'd clipped it and ironically it was the set of knives that he bought [me] and cut my throat with. (**Kya**)

> To my body, black eyes, I don't know how many times I used the story that I was changing the [light] bulb and it broke and the glass fell in my eye because I used to walk around with an eye patch and just make up stories about my eye. I had a crook eye and I was seeing the specialist and all this sort of jazz. (**Nia**)

Stolen Generations: Kima's story

Kima was in her fifties when we spoke. She was part of the Stolen Generations, one of the thousands of children who 'were forcibly removed by governments, churches and welfare bodies to be raised in institutions, fostered out or adopted by non-Indigenous families, nationally and internationally' (AISTSIS nd). Kima described her experiences of being removed from her Indigenous parents and placed into a non-Indigenous home, where, in her words, she 'became the property' of the non-Indigenous family:

> I was taken when I was four years old; it was via an adoption centre. But you sort of weren't adopted, you know what I mean, it was not supposed to be legal to take children then, so they were sort of fake adoptions if you like, to make it look legal. They weren't taking

> children but you were brought up with a white family and were sort of like a worker on their property. (**Kima**)

Kima's experiences created vulnerabilities in her adult relationships. Without stating that she was raped, Kima alludes to conceiving her children through forced sexual experiences.

> Well I [was] beat up, beat every day, because I had to be white, I had to be taught to be white ... The violence started as a child. Just being taken was violent. I was terrified of my parents, and I was four, like, I didn't even want to call them mum and dad because they weren't even the same colour [laugh]. We were also sexually abused by the man in that family ... I tried to speak out and wasn't believed, I was called a liar. I still struggle with that, because histories repeat. What you are subjected to as a child, if you don't resolve that, you take that into your adult relationships. Then you start wondering if you are a liar, you start questioning your sanity. You really don't know how to protect your children either. The way I had my children was through violence, they were to white men. (**Kima**)

As a teenager, Kima left her foster home with a man to escape from violence, and she fell pregnant. What happened next impacted her greatly. The man she had trusted to help her escape took her child — her daughter — without her knowledge. Kima and her daughter were separated for several years. When she attempted to reunite with her child, Kima's powers as a parent were removed through lies told by her former partner. Her voice was silenced. She had no mechanism of advocacy and was made to feel powerless. The removal of her child continued a multigenerational legacy of child removal. Her child was removed by the perpetrator (the child's biological father), not by the state, but the impact of the removal was no different from what she had experienced herself as a child.

> The people that adopted me, I was just disowned by them ... We didn't really talk [about] domestic violence, and not [about] sexual abuse. You couldn't say anything about black and white issues ... [As an adult] I was in a relationship which I was sort of like a hostage. He took my child; it was all just repeating. I swung between suicidal, homicidal, my emotions weren't being addressed; then having my child [taken,] that sort of mucks around with your bonding with them as well. I was 18 [laughs], it was horrific really. (**Kima**)

These experiences came at a cost to the mental health and wellbeing of both Kima and her daughter. Kima spoke about her own issues with substance misuse; because of the disconnect, her child also experienced substance misuse and anxiety. Kima said that such experiences have a ripple effect:

> I came home one day, and everything was gone, an empty shell of a house. My child was gone, everything in the house was gone and he was gone, the car that was it ... all gone. I have reconnected with the child, who now has major drug and alcohol issues, depression, anxiety issues. That all repeats, it doesn't just affect one person. (**Kima**)

Kima was eventually held responsible by her former partner for leaving him and their child. Her relationship had included multiple forms of violence, significant manipulation and coercive control, and caused a complete emotional and mental breakdown, which resulted in hospitalisation. At the time, she was homeless and living rough, and had sex with people in exchange for shelter. She became conditioned to believe the perpetrator's statements were true.

> I was just left in the streets. He tried to get me back and it was all about control, you know, [he said,] 'you've been a bad girl, you do

> what I want, and things will get better'. But from sitting in that gutter, I thought I would be [better off] in the gutter than being with him. Because mentally, physically, spiritually, emotionally, I was just imploding. Exploding! Like it was all just uncorking and unravelling. I couldn't go any further; I had a complete breakdown ... My husband turned out to be a stalker. He didn't think he'd lose control of me [laugh] like I was his little slave, so he was a bit miffed I suppose about having lost the battle. He kept it going and I felt like I was a rabbit being chased by a bloke with a gun. In those days, stalking wasn't illegal. [The perception of society was] it was okay, 'oh he cares about you, he loves you' and whilst you're trying not to go mental, you don't like being homeless, you don't like being an alcoholic or having to sleep with people for a bed to sleep in or a roof over your head. You start thinking the way other people tell you to think, you know, instead of listening to in here [pointing to her chest]. (**Kima**)

Violence in a LGBTQIA+ relationship—Adira's story

Violence can affect Indigenous women in any relationship, not just heterosexual relationships. Adira experienced coercive control in a same-sex relationship. She shared her experiences of having her power taken away when her partner made her choose between playing sport, which was her passion, or being in a relationship.

> In my first relationship, I suffered from depression, bad anxiety, abuse. I was with her for about 10 years ... I had everything going for me, I had a [sporting] career, I was playing representative sport by the time I was ... 11 ... And then I got picked to go overseas at the age of 17 ... I met someone at the age of 18 and then my life just changed from there. I let everything go. She made me choose, either her or my [sport] and I chose her because I didn't know at the time. A year into

> it was good, but then I felt like I was pushing my family away, and then I ended up moving [relocating] at the age of 19. I wasn't in control of myself, I felt like she had control of everything and it was her way or no way. I've never been abused in my entire life, like being, bullied, being hit by another person. Being controlled [in] everything I did, it wasn't right. I think the last thing she did was when she pushed me down the stairs and ... because I suffer from epilepsy, when she pushed me down the stairs I had a big fit and that's when I knew it was enough.
>
> After six months, she wanted to try and work it out so I gave her a second chance. But when I caught her cheating, that just made [me] realise that I was better off without her so I just walked, I didn't do anything. I finally had the strength to just [say], 'no more'. (**Adira**)

I asked Adira about her confidence in formalised violence orders or court processes and whether she considered reporting the violence.

> I never believed in that kind of stuff because, I don't know, maybe call me old school, but I felt like why I should get the police involved ... I know they're there for protection and stuff like that but where were they ... like back in the old days [for] women like us? Indigenous women had to find strength to get past their suffering, they had to find their own strength. So why do I need a police officer to tell me that I need a piece of paper to show that I'm stronger than a person when I can just show that I am, but in my own little way. (**Adira**)

Adira said that her sister, who was in a heterosexual relationship, experienced physical violence and followed advice from their parents, who had raised them not to accept any form of abuse. However, Adira felt that her experience was different because she was in a same-sex relationship and experienced ongoing coercive control, which can be difficult to recognise.

She was self-reflective, and said she left the relationship when she could — which was when she realised that the patterns in her partner's behaviour were unhealthy.

> Well, my sister went through it. I saw it but I think she had got abused for the first time, she walked that first day and I saw it and that was scary. She just ... she had moved in with her high-school lover and they had a kid and then he came home one night from footy, and he abused her in the kitchen. I've never seen my sister be so strong like that, but the first hit, the first abuse was the last. I should have been strong enough like that, like our parents told us, nothing should ever ... no one should ever do that to you and ... but I had it constantly. **(Adira)**

Adira's family knew she was experiencing difficulties in her relationship. They didn't intervene, but she knew they were watching and understood what was happening. It's possible her family held back so that Adira and her partner could work through issues together, and she knew that if she needed their support they would have helped.

> My mum knew, she never said anything, but she knew because all she would say to me, 'I know you don't have to say anything, I see it.' My best friend, my brother and my sister, just my family, they knew. **(Adira)**

Childhood violence

Several of the women I spoke to had experienced childhood trauma — also known as adverse childhood experiences, which include witnessing violence between parents and other family members, experiencing violence and experiencing child sexual assault.

Tesha spoke of childhood sexual abuse. Although she reported it to the police, she experienced fear about the possible repercussions for her family. The stigma of shame continues to impact our communities and makes it difficult for people to speak about these experiences.

> Back then it was sort of like … a shame job, like you just didn't tell them what the problem was, you didn't say, it was like you don't want that coming out. I feared what it would do to my family, and it just wasn't cool, like it wasn't sort of spoke of. I reported it, I went to court. But it took me a while to get my strength. I … got to the stage where I went, well, I must stand strong, I don't want my children thinking it's okay for that sort of behaviour to happen. (**Tesha**)

Fear, stigma and threats of repercussions are some of the greatest challenges in reporting violence. Most of the women and families referred to threats about what would happen if they shared their stories.

CHAPTER 4

SEMICOLON (;) – MY STORY

Project Semicolon is an international movement that presents hope to people who are struggling with depression, suicide, addiction and self-injury.[1] I've come to see the semicolon as an important symbol in my life. Rape, sexual assault and violence are part of my story, which I tell here. So is a suicide attempt.

MY JOURNEY IN TERMS OF VIOLENCE

There's been different violence in my life. I would say from my earliest memories in my life, they have been very traumatic. Witnessing violence from my biological father and what he did to my mother. But also, as a child being sexually abused, over several years by different people. It started from about when I was four, right up until I was 15. I was 15 when the last incident happened, where I was raped. I haven't reported it because it's too far away in my memory. There's not enough evidence to go to court, because my memory is blank. I've just got black spots. It's like my brain has closed off those memories, I can't really remember what happened in terms of how it happened or what I did to fight him off

1 See the Project Semicolon website (https://projectsemicolon.com/) for more information.

or whatever. It's frustrating because I just can't remember. I know it was not consensual. I have racked my brain for years just trying to remember what happened.

… after being raped I attempted suicide. I took a whole lot of tablets. The night I attempted suicide, it must have been a Sunday night. The next day, when I woke up, mum was there telling me get up to go to school. I couldn't wake up properly; I was groggy for about three days straight. At that point in time of my life, I just wanted to take those tablets and go to sleep. When I think back to it now, I'm just glad I woke up.

From my earliest memories, I recall violence being perpetrated against my mother. My sister was only young, maybe two or three, so she may not remember these events. However, I remember them vividly. I also remember witnessing violence towards other family members. During this period when my mum experienced violence, I was being sexually abused by a non-Aboriginal friend of the family. I was only about four or five when it started.

For me, the sexual violence didn't stop here. I experienced further abuse throughout my childhood, from different people at different times. When I was just about to turn 12, I was raped by my mother's former partner. I was in Year 6, still in primary school. I told a friend that I had been sexually assaulted. She told her mother, who then told the school. On the Monday, I was removed from class and taken for a medical examination.

The medical examination was a traumatic experience. My memories of it are patchy, but some things are etched in my mind. I remember the cold wooden bench covered with a type of lino material. I had to lie on it. I remember the bench was near a window and the roller curtain was pulled down. I remember the doctor, a male, telling me to take down my underwear, lie on the table and put my legs in the stirrups. The stirrups were cold hard plastic. Most of all, I remember the bright light that was used for the internal examination.

I felt scared, and my body was exposed. I remember questions running through my mind. Who was this person? He was a stranger, and I didn't know if I could trust him. The examination was traumatic — especially as the cold instruments were inserted into my body to check if there was any damage. I closed my eyes and took myself far away. I know now that I dissociated. Dissociating became my way of dealing with all violence.

Since that medical examination, I find it difficult not to experience negative thoughts in similar examinations, like pap smears or anything with a bright light. Even today, I must remind myself that what I'm experiencing is not the same as (or because of) 'that' procedure I had as an 11-year-old.

My experiences of sexual assault didn't stop here. I was raped again when I was 15, and that's when I attempted suicide. I felt so alone and isolated — as though there was no one I could turn to. I felt that any time I believed I could trust someone, they turned out to be another perpetrator — or a survivor themselves. I had no idea who to speak to, so I overdosed on my mum's medication.

After that experience, I wagged a lot of school and began to drink a lot of alcohol. I even ran away from home, and the police in Sydney tracked me down. I didn't tell the police about the rape, and I didn't tell anyone about my suicide attempt. No one knew. I was displaying trauma-related coping mechanisms, but they were not picked up.

The man who assaulted me as a four-year-old has passed, and I had nothing more to do with him after those days. At the time, his wife was my babysitter and they lived around the corner from our family home. I don't know who decided that my sister and I would not return to that house — I haven't asked my mum.

The man who sexually assaulted and raped me between the ages of eight and 11 has also passed. I did go through a court procedure in response to his abuse. I provided a detailed statement, and he ultimately confessed. He got jail time in New South Wales. Because he was convicted of incidents in two different states, he first had to serve his time in New South Wales, then proceed with matters in Victoria. He was living in a halfway house before starting the proceedings in Victoria. However, three days before he was due to appear in a Victorian court, he died by suicide.

And the third man who raped me is still alive. I have nothing to do with him and my memory of the event is blurry. It's as though my brain has repressed the memories. After studying psychology, I now understand that the brain protects us by repressing memories. I know I did not give consent to this man. But since I cannot recall specific moments, there is not enough evidence to proceed through court.

My experiences of violence did not stop here. I have also experienced violence in adult intimate relationships — including physical, verbal, emotional and psychological abuse, and coercive control. For many years I was hurt and angry. I behaved in a reactive way towards the person who used violence against me. However, when I returned to Australia after living overseas for some time, I decided I had to speak to the perpetrator about the violence I had experienced. This process was not easy. I had been carrying a lot of hurt and pain for many years. When we finally spoke, I would get to a point in the discussion where I had to stop and leave. Sometimes I got angry and said horrible things. To his credit, he stayed in those meetings and owned his behaviours. We reached a point where he needed to own his behaviour and subsequent actions so that I could move forward. During this process, I had the time and space to manage my emotions, thoughts and feelings. I recognise that not everyone can get to this point — for many different reasons. I'm sharing that this worked for me. Where it is safe to do so, it can work.

CHAPTER 5

KIRSTY'S STORY – OPERATION GET HOME

In the next few pages, I share the story of my cousin Kirsty, who gave me permission to share some experiences from an incident that occurred while she was overseas on holiday. I use her real name as she specifically stated that she wanted some of her story shared. Another cousin of ours, Bud, is also part of this story and has also given permission for his real name to be used.

Kirsty is a beautiful woman with a massive heart. She is a mother of three and a business owner. While Kirsty was overseas, Bud and I were in contact with her through social media. Kirsty was with her then-partner, whom she'd met after separating from her children's father. They were away for a three-week tropical holiday.

I hadn't met this guy and, to be honest, I'm now glad I never did.

Kirsty and her partner were doing what tourists do, enjoying their holidays. Kirsty used social media to share pictures and posts about the holiday, and I often added comments privately on the story as Kirsty would post them. On one picture, I asked about the rain and whether there had been a break in the weather. But something about Kirsty's reply seemed off.

Marlene: Geez is it still raining?

Kirsty: Next time I travel, I travel with someone who isn't a cunt. Full stop.

Marlene: Oh shit. This your new man?

Kirsty: Yep. Asshole. Enough said.

Marlene: You safe though?

Kirsty: No. I'm stuck here, scared fucking shitless sissy. I don't know what to do. I'll go outside and send you everything. Hang on.

I had sent those three important words: *You safe though?* My protective instinct had kicked in and I knew something was very wrong. Later, Bud and I eventually understood what had happened, and Kirsty sent pictures and videos of the bruises and injuries. She ended up with extensive injuries, all over her body and internally.

Kirsty told me that during the first week of the holidays, something happened one night and her partner snapped. He was highly intoxicated and he physically assaulted Kirsty. He kicked and trod on her, dragged her, threw her up a stairwell, rammed her head into a wall, and then threw her around the hallway outside their motel room. He also shouted at her and verbally abused her. She remembers some of what happened, but she was knocked unconscious from the violence.

I won't go into specific details, as I don't want to write something that will create flashbacks for Kirsty. But when I saw the videos she sent of her injuries, it was impossible not to get upset. I called Bud to find out if he knew anything. Bud and Kirsty have always been close, so I figured that if anyone knew what was going on, it would be him. We mobilised and started to arrange for Kirsty to come home, with Bud, Kirsty and me communicating through a three-way chat.

To make things worse, Kirsty had to share a room with this man for about 48 hours after the incident. For me, this was one of the scariest periods of my life. At first, Bud and I kept things quiet and didn't tell other people in the family. Then we spoke to Kirsty's ex-husband, who was just as concerned as us. We all mobilised to get her home ASAP! We put Operation Get Home into full effect.

While we worked to get Kirsty home, our only form of communication was text messages. We knew that phone calls would set him off. We waited to hear from Kirsty at times when she could message discreetly. She sent us snippets about what was happening in the room at the time, and we replied when we could. Bud and I always ended our messages with a 'delete' reminder for Kirsty, because she needed to be sure there was no evidence left on her phone. We kept the messages on our end. We knew the situation was volatile and were worried that he could easily do more harm to her.

I include excerpts of the messages between us in the next few pages (again, with Kirsty's and Bud's permission).

Kirsty: He's asleep again. Thought I'd just let you both know before going to sleep that I'm ok. I'll send a C throughout the night so when you wake you know I'm still ok. Love you both so much. X

Marlene: Glad you're ok(ish). How's the room situation?

Kirsty: I'll sleep here tonight. They've put security at my door. He knows it's there. The manager told him for my safety that they want to have security here. One more sleep and I'll get my ass to the airport when he goes out tomorrow.

Marlene: Have you got your passport and ID in a location you can quickly grab and go?

Kirsty: I left it with reception so he can't hide it. I can get it as soon as I go down there.

Marlene: Perfect, that's a good plan.

Bud: Delete.

In another series of text messages, Kirsty shared the details of her injuries and noted their locations on her body. They were all in places where they could be hidden by clothing.

Kirsty: Marks in all places that can be covered or not easily seen. He knew what he was doing.

Bud: Yep, rough you up enough to hurt you but not for it to be glaringly obvious.

Kirsty: He did stomp on my hand though. The manager confirmed that and said the lady next door seen him do it after he threw me headfirst into the wall in the hallway. Apparently, I was unconscious, and he kept yelling at me.

Marlene: Oh bub.

Bud: Fuck! Calculated, sly and a complete dog act!

Marlene: Delete.

During this process, both Bud and I were working in the background, making calls and getting advice. I had no idea how to get anyone out of a foreign country and away from this situation. We relied on people we knew for advice. I leaned on friends who were former police officers. Bud leaned on people he knew who had experienced violence. We all hoped the foreign authorities and the motel she was staying at would take care of Kirsty.

Bud: Did you delete your insta [Instagram] chat?

Kirsty: Yep, I delete everything as soon as I send it. The yelling and screaming at me has not stopped to be honest. Actually no. For about 5 hours yesterday he was nice.

Bud: What about?

Kirsty: Just about everything. Today he's been quiet and then he'll come back and have a go about something. I had the feeling something would turn to shit.

Bud: He fooled us all sis, don't stress it's not your fault, he's a professional at manipulating. Next time we just don't trust as easily.

Marlene: Delete.

The last 24 hours of Kirsty's time away were probably the most nerve-racking. I didn't sleep. I couldn't sleep, knowing that Kirsty was so far from home and unsafe. When we received messages from Kirsty, sometimes they seemed written as though she was speaking to herself. We supported her through these moments and made sure she knew we were right there with her. We weren't there in person, but she knew we were on the other end of the text messages.

Kirsty: 24 hours. We can do 24 more hours.

Bud: You've got a plan. You'll be safe and will start to heal. It's about you now. I got you. Marl has got you. But most importantly you've got yourself.

Kirsty: [I'm being] quiet, submissive, polite, nice. Keep myself safe!

Marlene: This is survival mode.

Bud: Play the game.

Marlene: Play it this way till you're out of there. Safety first.

Kirsty: If I need help security is there, and they have a key to access my room if needed. He [security] has my number. So sends a message every half hour just with a ? I send back a C. I'm going to sleep now. The more I sleep the quicker I get on that plane. I love you both sooo much. X

Bud: Good night love you. Delete.

The next morning, we again waited for messages from Kirsty. Her partner had become suspicious about who she was contacting back home.

We had to wait every time she messaged to know that she was ready to delete our messages.

> **Kirsty:** I'm hoping he fucks off on a scooter today.
>
> **Bud:** Can you pay the security to take you to the Australian embassy?
>
> **Marlene:** Might need a strategy for you, if he doesn't leave the room.
>
> **Kirsty:** I just asked security when I'm ready to go if they can take me and they said yes. He [security guard] has been there since 4pm [yesterday].
>
> **Bud:** Delete.

With the help of motel security and the local police, Kirsty was able to leave the room while her partner was out. Whether he knew about her plans, we don't know. I'm sure he would have known that her family would not leave her in a foreign country in a time of such need. Knowing that our cousin was leaving a situation where she could have been killed and with us possibly recovering her body was challenging for me — something I never thought I'd have to think about. That was my gravest fear, but my main concern was for her safety and getting her home to her children.

As the day went on, it was difficult for me to focus on work. I couldn't focus on anything really. I had the phone by my side and made sure I didn't go to sleep until I knew she was safe on the plane.

> **Kirsty:** I'm anxious, but so excited to be almost gone. Nearly there.
>
> **Marlene:** Acknowledge it. Move thru the thought. And move on. Focus on getting home. Breathe.
>
> **Bud:** You're going to feel so much more relaxed when you're on that flight. Still a few things to get there yet.

We finally received the messages we'd been waiting to read. She had mobilised. She had left the room. Then she left the motel. She had a police escort to the airport.

Kirsty: Leaving room now.

Kirsty: Nearly there.

Kirsty: About to get in car.

Marlene: Got passport?

Kirsty: In the car. Just left. All is good.

Bud: Awesome.

Marlene: The police there behind you?

Kirsty: Yes. Thank you both so much for everything.

Marlene: No thanks needed. We're family. Having you home with your kids, alive, is all that matters. A hug when I see you will be all I need.

Bud: You've been there for me and I'm sure you'd be there for Marl at the drop of a hat.

In times of hardship — like this situation with Kirsty — my family often relied on humour. Even as Kirsty was going through this crisis, we were able to share a joke. We knew each other well and had enough connection to see a shared joke even in a text message. In situations like this, a little humour goes a long way.

Kirsty: I'm in [country], in 35 degree heat, in tracksuit pants and a hoodie.

Marlene: Esshaaaay.

Kirsty: Yep. Tittie sweat I tell ya. And sister the humidity is crazy. Your hair would be so bad here. Especially with rain and humidity. I've been a mess and have had no clue at all this whole damn time.

Marlene: You are amazing. You have got out! Do you realise the strength and courage it takes to do that? That's enormous.

Kirsty: No I didn't. I been on auto pilot I think and have just had one goal, get home to my kids.

Bud: You had the courage to see what was going on. The strength to act on it and more importantly, listened to those that wanted to help you. You're a fuckn rockstar sis!!!

Kirsty's holiday happened in 2022. She arrived home safely, but it wasn't the end of her ordeal. Her ex-husband collected her from the airport. Like us, he was grateful she was home. But once she was home, reflection and reality hit — along with extreme panic attacks, severe post-traumatic stress disorder, anxiety and confusion. She then had to endure medical assessments, scans and x-rays. She has not proceeded with legal intervention — yet. It is too harrowing for her to relive and retell her story. Bud and I continue to support her, in all ways. When and if she decides to proceed with legal action, Bud and I and her ex-husband will all be there with her.

CHAPTER 6

THE DECISION TO LEAVE VIOLENCE – OR TO STAY

Attempting to leave an abuser can bring risks. Women who express their intent to leave a violent partner may exacerbate the severity of violence and significantly increase the potential risk of death, not only for themselves but potentially also for children. We need to reframe societal misconceptions and recognise that survivors may be strategically planning their departure from abusive situations. This process requires time, resources and support. Acknowledging these complexities is essential for providing effective support and ensuring the safety of Indigenous women.

When the women I spoke to reflected on staying in violent situations longer than they would have liked, they used self-critical language. However, their stories about what they did and how they left signalled to me that they were remarkably strong and capable, and I invariably interpreted their stories as strength-based ways of enacting agency.

SOMETIMES LEAVING SEEMS SIMPLER THAN IT REALLY IS ...

The perception that Indigenous women tolerate, accept, return to and stay in violent relationships is widespread. Women who choose to stay in violent situations do so for many reasons. Often threats to their children's safety or to other family members are core concerns.

> Like nearly every day I was getting hit but I was only worried that he'd do something to my daughter… I was worried that he'd try and take her. (**Lani**)

'Stuck in that cycle'

There's a widespread view that women get stuck in cycles of leaving and returning to a violent relationship (Stark 2013). But these situations are always complex, with survivors often feeling trapped with nowhere to turn — a feeling that's easily dismissed if the cycle of violence is accepted as the norm. The women I spoke to described many intersecting links — including links to their children, being caught in a cycle of believing change would occur only to discover that the perpetrator soon reverted to old behaviours, being caught up emotionally, and not understanding they were living in a cycle. Women described believing that they loved the perpetrator, even while their self-worth was being eroded.

Returning to violent situations often involves a promise that the relationship will be different. The perpetrator promises to change, but does not. In Jaylah's situation, the perpetrator used coercion to reconnect with her. She experienced manipulation as a means of bringing her back and, like many other perpetrators, her partner promised to change.

> He ended up coming around and conning me in, saying, come back, I won't hit you again, all that sort of thing and so I went back and, pretty well, it was the same.
>
> …
>
> He had a way of trying to make you feel guilty and he put a sorry act on, say things like, 'oh, I'm missing you, I'm missing our child' or 'I just want us to be together as a family' and then I'd be, like, well, come home to your family then, so I was stuck in that cycle. (**Jaylah**)

Jemila shared an interesting idea. She called her car her third space. This was the place where she would process the violence she experienced and safely gather her composure to help her brave the next part of her day. The process of stepping out of the car and closing the door was what I consider the liminal space.

> [W]hen I hit that [workplace] and I got out of my car, it was like the door closed and I became that happy [person] at work that had to be in control at work. (Jemila)

The women expressed their wish for people outside the relationship to take some time to examine the situation and speak to them about it. When a woman becomes isolated by the person who uses violence, it is difficult for her to seek help. Malia made a strong point about what influenced her to stay.

> It would be awesome if people could understand how hard it is to be on the other side. I've never been stupid, I've never been brought up around violence, I was always educated ... And yet people just think that you're stupid because you put up with it. But behind every decision there's a whole bunch of reasons *why* that person is choosing that decision. If you just take the time to listen to someone's reasons of why they're making that decision, you find out a whole heap more. For example, my reasons were I was that fearful for my family's safety and I just couldn't, I couldn't bring myself to leave. If people just stop and just take the time to think okay, it's not because they're just stupid that they're staying with someone that's in this domestic violence relationship, it's because they've got a whole heap of issues and they don't know how to reach out and find solutions for these issues. And if Indigenous women could just know that no one's the same but for every single Indigenous girl out there, if they're experiencing domestic violence no matter how many issues they've got that's making

them stay with someone that's hurting them, there's a whole heap of solutions if you can just sit down with someone and reach out and let the right people help you in the right way. You don't need to keep putting up with it. You're never alone. (**Malia**)

Negative social responses – judgement

There is a lot of judgement for women who speak up. There's a belief that their story won't be valued or heard or believed. And that's sad because there's a lot of women that are hurting and they should be believed ... A perpetrator will have the community and the family wrapped around their finger, that's what a perpetrator does. I hid it all those years. So, to do that it must mean I'm strong. To hide that stuff from other people took a lot of strength. It also took a lot of strength to leave him. I got to a point where I got fed up. So how do you build yourself back up? Slowly, through good people being around me [sniffles], just a day at a time. (**Jaylah**)

When Indigenous women in violent relationships are viewed through a lens of judgement, society often perceives their choice to remain with an abusive partner as a lack of agency. For example, child protection authorities may assert that women cannot regain custody of their children if they 'choose' to stay with a violent partner. As Jemila experienced, such perspectives oversimplify the complexities of intimate relationships. Preparing to leave requires planning and being ready to act. Jemila talked about how the lead-up stages took time. She experienced difficulty leaving in the face of judgemental attitudes — including judgement for choosing to stay in the relationship for so long.

You can't just get up and leave, you must leave when you're ready and sometimes that can take weeks, months or even years, but women, particularly women and not just Indigenous women, are highly

> judgemental. Highly judgemental on, not that we've left, but why didn't you leave earlier? ...
>
> I think women need to give other women a break, seriously. I mean everybody, I mean your family, your mothers or anything. We are already judgemental on ourselves, but we are judgemental on other women: 'why do [you] stay?', 'why do you put up with that?' (**Jemila**)

Approaching a stranger for help can be daunting, especially when Indigenous women are already in a vulnerable situation and feel they could be further judged when seeking help.

> How do I approach a stranger at a police station and divulge this information without being judged or, you know, [when they ask questions like] why don't you just leave the relationship, why don't you just leave the man, like it's not that easy just to leave. (**Jemila**)

When to stay and when to go—Jemila's story

It is a misconception to suggest that women choose to stay in abusive environments because they want to stay. Often, remaining is the safest option. Research indicates that women are at a higher risk of being killed after leaving a violent partner or expressing a desire to end a relationship. Leaving is rarely straightforward, as survivors face multiple threats — to their own safety, to the safety of their children and to the safety of family members and pets.

Jemila talked about the reality of living with daily violence and the choices she made to keep her children safe. She believed that it was safer for her children for her to stay in the relationship and let herself be the focus of his violence, not her children.

> I've lived it, I've breathed it, I've felt it and I've had to make the hard choices but they [society] don't understand that, *that* woman, in *that*

> house is doing whatever she can to keep her kids safe, and her breathing. Because while ever she's breathing those kids are safe because she'll take it, not the kids, and they [society] don't understand that. (**Jemila**)

Jemila described her experience of living in a violent situation and experiencing the perpetrator's power and control. One significant factor that contributed to her decision to stay was the perpetrator's threats to kill her children. Acknowledging this situation does not mean empathising with the aggressor, but it does involve understanding his behaviours and Jemila's need to keep her children safe. The fear and control that a perpetrator holds over a survivor, especially when children's lives are threatened, cannot be overstated. Jemila was acutely aware of the potential consequences, and this kept her from leaving.

> I never left, because the threat ... to kill my kids was enough for me to stay. If I knew then what I know now, I would have left a very long time ago. If I knew my kids were hearing it and hiding and frightened, I would have left a long time ago. (**Jemila**)

Having children with a violent partner creates additional layers of difficulty. Jemila knew that leaving would initiate further battles, including family law matters regarding custody. In her situation, it seemed safer to remain in the relationship while she planned her exit. However, Jemila recognised that the violence would escalate when she attempted to leave.

> Then all hell breaks loose. You thought it was bad before, no, that's when it's dangerous, when you've left that house, you have got a bigger target on [your] back ... because it's not just him, it's his friends, his family, it's everybody and he's the victim, you've left him. (**Jemila**)

Jemila described how her perpetrator eroded her self-worth, self-esteem and confidence — which all impacted her ability to decide to leave. Only after leaving the violence could she reflect on what had transpired and how it affected both her and her children.

> Because when you're in a domestic violence relationship, you don't have the self-worth and you don't think you can do it. You don't think you're capable of leaving. But I found that when I did leave, I had a lot of time to think ... but I realised I was doing myself a disservice, I was just going round, round, round in my head when I was in that relationship. (**Jemila**)

Jemila recognised that she needed resources and support if she was to leave safely with her children. She understood that the violence could continue if she stayed, and she understood the potential impact on her children. Importantly, she realised that the danger would increase if her partner discovered her intentions to leave.

Jemila was the primary income earner but she faced additional challenges because the perpetrator controlled her finances, necessitating stealth in saving for a rental housing deposit (bond) and household items to start anew. She acted in her children's best interests, prioritising their safety and survival while she planned and saved. Any suggestion that women who experience violence fail to protect their children undermines their agency and decision-making and ignores the active ways they prioritise their children's safety.

> The hard thing, how you get ready must be on an individual basis ... It depends on the violence that you're suffering, and it depends on the support system you have or what's available to you. See I was really lucky because I had a permanent job, the money went when I went, I wasn't a person that depended financially on him, he depended on

> me so my situation is a lot different. I had a job, I had money, you know, I only had to wait four weeks and I had my own bond. (**Jemila**)

Jemila was self-reliant, so her time of crisis and need for intervention support was brief—just for a few weeks until she could afford the bond for a new place to live. Leaving always requires planning, and Jemila's experience reinforces the need for workplace policies that include paid leave for domestic violence. Without the financial means to leave, she may have stayed longer than she did, putting herself and her children at further risk.

Financial control

Financial control by the perpetrator can make it difficult to leave. As Darrabarra said:

> He had me so controlled financially. He controlled where I could go. I couldn't go anywhere unless I had the kids with me. (**Darrabarra**)

Kima said that the system disenables the survivor and discourages them from seeking help. While she wasn't specific in her comment, she could be referring to equity in pay, which would provide women who work with sufficient financial resources to support themselves if they choose to leave. Indigenous women who are financially dependent on a perpetrator may decide to return to that perpetrator or immediately start a new relationship because they need financial support.

> Well, first up, I do believe that women's pay should be made [available] that if they need to leave violence that they can provide for their family on their own and instead of having to go and get another man to provide for them. Like, stop bagging out the women and telling them they're stupid when the system doesn't even make it possible for them to do that because a lot more of them would be doing it if it were possible. (**Kima**)

When a woman who is experiencing violence relies on the perpetrator, particularly for financial support, the likelihood that she'll return to the relationship increases. I want you, the reader, to understand — without judgement — that leaving a violent relationship can take many attempts. A woman may need to plan when and how to leave, while also factoring in her need for money to access safe housing. Leaving a violent person can be extremely scary, and can be hampered by people who are unaware of the need for confidentiality as a safety mechanism. This includes service providers, who may unknowingly compromise a woman's safety.

The breaking point

I asked women to describe the moment or point at which they made the decision to leave. I wanted to understand their breaking point and what was happening when they finally made the decision. Most of the women could identify where and when their moment of realisation occurred, and could describe their thought processes in deciding to leave. For Jemila, education and access to information were important, and they helped her to stand firm in her decision.

> I did try to leave and we did have breakups along the way but I kept going back to that relationship and then with education and information and last time that the assault happened that was the straw and I made a stance and said, that's not what I want, it's not good for the kids, it's not good for anyone and I was able to stick with that, but that was really tough for me too because I didn't get any support at all. (**Jemila**)

Children were a key motivator.

> I left many times. The point when I first left is that he threatened to kill me and the kids ... I said, 'No, fuck this, enough's enough, I can't deal with your fucking shit any more', and so I left him. (**Lani**)

For many of the women, leaving involved safety planning and finding safe places and services. Malia had her own income and was able to save money. Once she had saved enough, she found another house for herself and her daughter. However, the perpetrator found her:

> I started renting another house and got away from him and everything was okay until he found out where I was living ... He tried to kidnap [our daughter], bashed me again, smashed up the house I was in, smashed up my car, so I went to the police and started going through family law court and got orders against him. (**Malia**)

Jaylah reflected on a pivotal moment that prompted her to leave a violent relationship:

> The last time he put his hand on me [was] the reason why I got out ... We were [arguing and] standing in between the kitchen and the lounge room and I'm thinking to myself, where's a knife, I'm going to stab this cunt. That's when I realised, I've got to get out of this. It was that thought that scared me the most. It was — he's going to kill me, but I'm going to kill him before he kills me. I jumped in the car and I [went for a drive]. I just sat in the car near the water for maybe, I don't know, six or seven hours. When I came home, nothing was said. Again, that was the cycle ... Our cycle. [But] I had to hold my shit together because I've got kids and a responsible job. (**Jaylah**)

In that moment of desperation, Jaylah recognised the imminent danger she faced. She drove to a safe location where she could self-regulate and contemplate her next steps. Despite her inner turmoil, Jaylah concealed the violence from her children, her workplace and her community. Her desire for self-preservation became the turning point; after years of enduring abuse, she understood that staying could lead to a tragic outcome — imprisonment or death. Fortunately, Jaylah removed herself from the situation and regained control over her emotions. She listened to what was a wake-up call about the years of violence she had endured. Her experience illustrates the hidden struggles of many Indigenous women, who often endure violence in silence and feel unable to reveal their circumstances to those around them.

For some women, the violence they experienced escalated when they left or informed the perpetrator they wanted to end the relationship. The result for the women was a state of hypervigilance — a combination of recovering from violence and expecting more violence, while planning and securing accommodation and financial assistance, and managing potential involvement of child protection if the police are alerted.

> While ever you're there putting up with it, they think it's their right to do what they want to do but when you've gone, who else are they going to take it [out] on, they don't want to hit the wall, they don't want to go and hit a punching bag, they don't want to kick the living daylights out of your car. They want to hurt you for not being there as their stress release. But if you're not there for that stress release they don't cope and that's the most scary part. (**Jemila**)

> I eventually gained the will to walk away, that was my last stint after I'd come back from the refuge, he'd found us, my son had given us up. He told my mum and my mum told him [the perpetrator]. I didn't tell my mum where I was going, what I was doing, nothing because I knew it would get back to the community and get back to someone in the family for him. So yeah, that was a bit of an eye opener. He found us, he came to the refuge, got us and we ended up coming home with him, I gave in. That night he flogged me with a fucken fence paling, so I've basically picked up the kids and ran and just hitchhiked basically home, back to my mum and dad's and that was enough. I just drew the line that day. (**Nia**)

THE NEED TO SUPPORT WOMEN TO LEAVE VIOLENCE

As described throughout this book, responses from service providers can significantly hinder Indigenous women's access to assistance when they seek safety from violence. Service providers' responses can be both positive and negative, and can function as a barrier or a motivator for women in need. Negative social responses can discourage Indigenous women from seeking help.

> I've heard from other women that they've reported violence and because they don't have a bruise or they don't have a cut or they're not up in hospital beat up bad, that the police have actually said, 'if only you came in with some sort of bruise on your body or something like that', as if that's the validation for violence, that it has to be something physical and something seen. But when you're in this [relationship] and it's psychological and if you're acting out, you're labelled irrational, and then you get locked up because you're going off your head because you've been psychologically abused. Perpetrators know how to manipulate the system. These people know the system when they've been in it and around it for long enough. **(Jaylah)**

The women and families I spoke to all described thoughts and feelings about being trapped, having nowhere to turn, and being isolated or dismissed if they reached out for assistance. Of the women who experienced non-physical violence, many were not aware that what they had experienced would be described as violence.

As Malia describes, Indigenous women find it extremely difficult to report violence, so the first responder is often a family member. Malia shared her experiences of engaging with the support system, where her interactions required code-switching in communication methods and language and knowing when to engage and when to remain quiet. She felt she needed to know what to say and what not to say. This code-switching occurs daily for Indigenous people, particularly those who seek support.

> I did not ever trust the justice system for me, they didn't want me to be alive; they weren't going to help me survive, so I would never go near a policeman, never go near a court. They did not have my interest at heart and I'm not stupid, like I do get sick of black being thought to be stupid, so for all you know it could be the other way around ... How somebody else's word, a white person's word, will be taken over mine ... because why? Because I'm Indigenous ... Like [if] a white woman couldn't even get the justice system to protect her, what hope did a black woman have? ... that's the reality of the justice system and then who's protecting our kids? Nobody. Like I said, I had to learn to be smart and I wasn't just going to go to talk to any old Tom, Dick and Harry ... Like I said, I didn't go near police. (**Malia**)

Community connectedness, confidentiality and fear of child removal

The women I spoke to carefully considered and planned their escapes. They were also mindful of the perpetrator's power, including the perpetrator's actions to that point and their potential future actions. Several women were concerned about whom they could trust. They questioned whether they could trust their own family and friends and considered whether the perpetrator's extended family and friends might talk about their plans to leave.

In Indigenous communities, interconnectedness and kinship structures are an added complexity and can create issues for women seeking help when they're experiencing violence. Kinship structures and extended family networks can be protective factors, but they can also create risk.

As Jemila described, 'you have got a target on your back'. Women need to consider the possibility of encountering family and friends of the perpetrator who may be employed in support services. They also need to consider issues around confidentiality in tight-knit communities. Having to navigate these issues can deter women from approaching services and seeking support. This can be particularly relevant for women who are planning to leave a relationship and need to develop a safety plan.

> People would know, confidentiality is not always confidential, right? And particularly, you know, we like to talk, blackfullas love to talk and people take their jobs very seriously but you only need to be seen to talk to one person and all of a sudden your whole life's been spread. (**Imani**)

Community connectedness is also relevant in terms of an Indigenous woman's own employment. If she works in a government or non-government service with mandatory reporting responsibilities, her situation becomes even more complicated. Knowing about mandatory reporting can influence a woman's willingness to seek support, and the risk of losing a child or children is a specific deterrent for many Indigenous women. For Imani, this was a reality. At the point of reporting the violence to police, Imani needed to notify her employer about the events to ensure her confidentiality. She was unsure about who might attend as responding officers when she called the police. She was concerned that her confidentiality could be compromised by colleagues in other agencies if they knew she was experiencing violence, and she was worried they would remove her child.

> I was sort of in the professional loop, so I guess conflict of interest, I was worried about as well because I didn't know who the professionals were going to be or even with the police. Because I'd worked with the police and having that fear around confidentiality, I was known 'cos of my job, that was a big thing for me. (**Imani**)

For most of the women I spoke to, the decision to report violence to police or other authorities was influenced by the risk of child removal. This was a particular concern when women wanted to reach out for support from service providers who had a reporting mandate. Many women were concerned that their children would be removed because they were exposed to violence. They also felt stress about being judged for staying with a person who used violence. They were worried they would be seen as placing their children in risky situations — in ways that placed the attention on the women, rather than on the people who used violence.

> [T]he amount of stress and the emphasis on the women, if police come and there's domestic violence, you're a bad mother, you're a bad woman, child protection might come and take your kids and all that sort of business, and the men always get away scot-free. **(Nia)**

When a child could be at risk of harm, it may be reported to child protection services. The risk of losing a child or children if the situation is reported by a mandatory reporter is a specific deterrent to women: it discourages them from seeking support. In addition, the women's identity can be at risk. For example, if an Indigenous woman is employed by a state agency and is experiencing violence, the mandatory reporting process may disclose her identity. Imani experienced this: when she reported the violence, she had to notify her employer about what was happening to ensure her confidentiality remained.

> So I guess there was a conflict of interest. I was worried, I didn't know who the professionals were going to be, or even in the police because I'd worked with the police and having that fear around confidentiality, that was a big thing for me. **(Imani)**

Some women experienced losing contact with their children through actions of a violent partner. Darrabarra experienced this, with two of her three children taken under what appears to be false pretences. Their father's family helped to keep the children away from her for well over nine months.

> He took them, and he kidnapped them. My daughter didn't go, the only reason being was because we had a sport tournament, and we had to be there. I said to him, 'you can have 'em for a few days, and then I'll meet you to pick them up.' And yeah, I was ringing, no answer, rang his mother, and she goes, 'no, I haven't heard from him.' Nine months. For nine months, I was a mess. I kept ringing his mother because she was our only point of contact. Then I went to the legal service and started the family court orders and all that sort of stuff. So, all this time I didn't know where my fucken kids were and they were at his mother's all the time, with their grandmother. The police found him and my children, so I went the next day and got them. They didn't want to come near me, they were so scared and I'm like, 'What's the matter?' They said, 'Dad told us you were killed, you were dead'. They were only two and three at the time. (**Darrabarra**)

A MESSAGE FROM JEMILA

Jemila's story shows that it can take several attempts for a woman to leave a violent partner. Each time a woman tries to leave, she has opportunities to discuss the situation and plan what is needed. While some people can leave immediately, for others it's a longer process of planning and building support networks that can swing into action when the woman decides it's time. It's vital that the support these women receive is both nonjudgemental and patient – leaving can take multiple attempts, and each should be seen as a genuine attempt to be safe and free of violence. Each attempt to leave is an effort of self-determination.

… we're not victims and that victim word has to go. We're survivors, whether we survive for one day and go back or not, we survived one day. It's not a waste of their time because we might not leave this time, but there'll be one time that we do leave, and it doesn't matter whether it takes 100 trips or not, it's like riding a bike. You might fall off it 100 times but soon you'll get it right. **(Jemila)**

CHAPTER 7

AFTERMATH: WAS IT LOVE?

Violence is fundamentally incompatible with genuine love. It is not a manifestation of care, respect or connection — values that underpin healthy relationships. In Indigenous communities (and other communities), the perception that violence can be a form of love is often rooted in toxic masculinity that manifests as dominance, control and aggression (Stark 2023). Furthermore, this distorted view may be linked to the honeymoon phase of the cycle of violence (Stark 2023; Innes and Anderson 2015; Walker 1980), where perpetrators often express remorse or affection after episodes of violence, perpetuating confusion and false associations between affection and violence.

The women tussled with the idea that there had been love in their relationships. While many were able to identify some moments that showed elements of their former partner's care for them, they also realised that the partner's behaviours were part of a cycle. For many, the cycle became clearer after they left the violent relationship and were able to reflect on what had happened. Often their partners' behaviours swung between what appeared to be love and care and what was clearly violence and disrespect.

For Lani, a cycle of violence and forgiveness extended over many years until she eventually realised she didn't need the perpetrator and found an inner strength by developing a strong mindset. The psychological abuse she survived is evident in the way she talks about her relationship with the person she thought she loved.

> Because you think you love him so much you forgive him, and so he would ring you, I'm sorry babe, I'm sorry that I done that to you, I'm sorry that I hurt you and me, being a fool, take him back and this happened over 11 years.
>
> ...
>
> I left him, like, I can't even count that many times but because I thought that I needed him, because I thought that I need him financially and emotionally and because I thought that you need to be there as a family, as a father because of the kids. But because you're in that state of mind, you just go back to them, you keep going back and back and back because you think that you need him. **(Lani)**

'Blackfulla love'

'Blackfulla love' is a common term in Indigenous communities and is used to describe a specific type of intimacy. While the exact usage may vary across the country, it's often used to refer to an Indigenous man who is violent one moment then seeks intimacy the next. The term functions as a euphemism or a type of figurative language that captures both the complexity and ugliness of these relationships. It signals a pattern where acts of violence are interpreted, either by the perpetrator or within community conversations, as part of love or emotional intimacy, and while it resonates as a cultural expression, it also carries risks. It can inadvertently perpetuate harmful stereotypes, suggesting that violence is an inherent or acceptable component of love within relationships.

Such narratives muddy the understanding of healthy love and normalise violence, thus reinforcing destructive cycles.

As an Indigenous slang term, I found no written record of 'blackfulla love' being used in Australia. However, one paper by Tehee and Esqueda (2008:30–33) uses the term 'Indian love' to describe this type of violence within relationships in Native American communities. Terms like 'blackfulla love' and 'Indian love' could be reinforced through the history of Western ideologies that saw Indigenous people branded as 'aggressive, violent, sexually promiscuous' (Loomba 2015:119). It could also be a demonstration of adaptation by Indigenous men, showing learned experiences of Western patriarchal ways, particularly white possessive logics and the perception of ownership of women (Moreton-Robinson 2015; hooks 1982).

Expressions like 'blackfulla love' and 'black velvet' function as an informal language that is heavily influenced by Western observers. Historically, Western discourse has used phrases like this to marginalise Indigenous women's experiences of violence, often positing violence as an element of love or passion. These concepts are rooted in stereotypes of Indigenous relationships as being inherently turbulent or dangerous.

When these terms are adopted and adapted within Indigenous communities, their meanings can shift and become sites of cultural expression, but the origins and implications remain complex. Such phrases often arise as a linguistic response to social marginalisation, yet are underpinned by Western frameworks that create and sustain representations of Indigenous love and violence. They tend to oversimplify the realities of Indigenous intimate relationships, perpetuating harmful stereotypes and obscuring the causes of violence and trauma. Consequently, they risk reducing complex emotional and cultural dynamics to reductive labels that may inadvertently reinforce damaging narratives. Instead of fostering understanding or healing, they exacerbate harm and misrepresent Indigenous experiences.

Phrases like 'blackfulla love' do not genuinely reflect love. Instead, they reveal the intersection of trauma, social stereotyping and linguistic construction. They gloss over the deep-rooted issues that underpin violence, including our colonial history and cultural dislocation. They perpetuate a narrative that conflates love with violence instead of challenging these harmful ideas.

To move toward healing, Indigenous communities and scholars need to challenge these narratives, deconstruct the origins of such terms and actively reclaim what love means on Indigenous terms. In this way, we can create new discourses that restore power, respect and agency while reshaping the language around love to reflect authentic understandings and promote loving connections.

Nia's story about 'black man's love'

In discussing the issue of intimacy shortly after experiencing violence, Nia shared her thoughts on what she called 'black man's love'. She recounted an experience involving an Indigenous man who was violent towards her and then sought intimacy shortly afterwards. She described this approach as, 'basically slapping them up, and saying, "I love you" after the fact. How is that love?' Her question strikes at the core of the misconception that violence and love can be intertwined. When I asked Nia to elaborate on what a black man's love meant to her, she described the situation in more detail.

> I wasn't allowed to work for a long time, so I was a stay-at-home mum, cleaning, cooking and entertaining his friends. The night that I got out of hospital from having bub, cos I had to have an emergency caesarean, I came home to him and all his mates having a massive party, all off their heads on drugs and alcohol ...
>
> When I was leaving him, [he would say things like] don't leave me, I love you, I'm sorry, I'll never do it again. It's all those little traits with, like I said, that black man's love unfortunately.
>
> ...

> Basically, slapping them up, and saying 'I love you' after the fact. How is that love? If someone's going to hurt you and then turn around and want to lay up with you, know what I mean, and it's just like no! You just bashed me, like, two hours ago [laugh] and now you want to lay up and make love to me, like what the fuck … Yeah, it was just weird conversation to have with him, you know, it was like … I couldn't bring it up with him. Like I said, I was always on eggshells. (**Nia**)

We need to be clear in our understanding: violence of any sort is not loving. To say that violence is somehow connected to the way that Indigenous men and women express their love is untrue. Any acceptance of violence can only lead to toxic masculinity and narcissism. We should not accept this in any relationship.

LIFE AFTER VIOLENCE – HYPERVIGILANCE, ANXIETY, STRESS

When I asked the women about life after violence, they spoke of residual impacts of anxiety and stress, including the need to stay on high alert — hypervigilance continues beyond the violent relationship.

> If there's a fight in public or a man raising his voice I get really nervous. If anybody starts getting aggressive towards me, even if they're not aggressive, if they just raise their voice in frustration and it's a bloke, I'll get nervous. (**Malia**)

> You have your good and bad days with it, some days you feel like it's unbearable, all the memories and the triggers and everything that goes with it, like it never leaves you, never, it's just about what measure it is for you at the time. (**Amahle**)

> There's stuff that I must deal with on a day-to-day basis like the anxiety, the [post-traumatic stress disorder], the issue with vulnerability and stuff like that. It's power, it's understanding who I am as a woman but it's also the other things, like I double-check the doors at home, I'm startled easily. I can't be in big crowds. I need space and time away from people a lot just to recharge, so it's kind of like there's a double edge to it as well. I've still got the anxiety, I've still got the touchiness, I've still got the insecurities, but at the end of the day, leaving was worth it. (**Jaylah**)

Jemila compared her experiences to living 'on death row':

> They [society] don't understand that the most vital time between you leaving and getting established … It's like as if you are on death row. You're not in danger while you live there and put up with it, you're in danger when you leave, and they [society] don't get it. They don't get it. They don't get it as in, that [while] he has control inside that house, he has control of you, the kids and everything. And all of that. But when you leave, you don't have control over your environment, you don't know where you are, you're always looking over your shoulders and they [the perpetrator] are at their worst. (**Jemila**)

Rebuilding self-worth and finding support in old and new relationships

For many women, being connected to a supportive network helps to support self-determination and gives women strength. The person who uses violence may attempt to isolate and fracture any supportive relationships but, as Lani noted, family can be a support network that helps women rebuild their self-worth and confidence.

> Having a strong family, having a strong support network, being strong within myself, building up my confidence and my strength mentally and emotionally, I could do that. **(Lani)**

For Jemila, rebuilding her self-worth was important. Her experiences in a violent relationship affected her future relationships — she needed to be with someone who understood the impact of violence.

> So, I went and joined the women-only gym and just went and just plodded around and lost weight and looked well and started looking after myself and then I found out that I am worth it and what you think or thought mattered a lot, but what others thought of me diminished the healthier I got.
>
> …
>
> But if you ever get another partner, they have to understand that, yes, okay, it's not rational to them but it's fuckin' rational to me and just ride the wave or shut up and go away and let me ride the wave because it's a long life disease. **(Jemila)**

Adira also discussed the way that previous experiences of violence stayed with her in subsequent relationships. When we spoke, she had been in a same-sex relationship for almost five years. Adira said the experience of her first relationship had changed her thinking. Now, she would not accept being controlled or treated in a way that was harmful or disrespectful. She felt she had found herself.

> You get into a new relationship [laughs] again and that kind of gets in the way of your job and that and after the first couple of months, jealousy kicks in with your new partner, but then you kind of just drift away. You're not going to let that happen again second time

> around, you put your foot down and you say, you support my situation, or you leave. (**Adira**)

When I asked Adira to describe what had changed, she was clear: she had learned that a healthy relationship needs communication, with both people working through issues together.

> I wasn't going to be a child no more, like you talk about it, you talk it over, you sit down, you don't run away from it and when you know that your other half has suffered as well, you kind of work together through that even though at the start, you're taking it out on each other, but you work through it and you get past it. (**Adira**)

HOLDING PERPETRATORS TO ACCOUNT – JAYLAH'S STORY

Perpetrators need to accept responsibility and accountability if we are to make any progress in addressing the violence experienced by Indigenous women. So often the survivor is the focus of attention and is blamed for the violence. Somehow, the person perpetrating the violence is absolved of responsibility or accountability, or, in Jaylah's case, absolves himself:

> I know what he's capable of and that fear was always in the back of my mind. I just didn't know what he would do ... Because he used to say to me, 'there's only one person that could kill me and you, and that's you', talking about me, more or less saying that if I didn't shut up he'd kill us both. (**Jaylah**)

Jaylah also described her frustration at community complicity and the ways men are not held to account for their violence. This is a community issue that requires *all* community members to stand up to perpetrators — especially community members who are related to the perpetrators. Without using the term, Jaylah discussed what is commonly called 'toxic masculinity' — that is, hypermasculine traits that are often harmful or negative (Innes and Anderson 2015).

> When I first went to a woman's shelter, the woman worker there questioned me about whether I was aware of the status of his family in the community. I wasn't sure if she was trying to confuse me any more than I already was, so I ignored what she said. I don't know what it is about men in our community, it's like they're put up on a pedestal and it's bullshit ... People don't say anything to the men in our community and no one stands up to them. Then when we do stand up and we talk, the focus is not on them, it's on the woman, or she's the one that started it. Now that's got to stop. (**Jaylah**)

CHAPTER 8

KNOW THEIR NAMES: FLORRIE REUBEN, CRYSTAL RATCLIFFE, ALLIRA GREEN AND BABY JAI

Florrie Reuben — a Torres Strait Islander and Aboriginal mother and grandmother; Crystal Ratcliffe and Allira Green — both Aboriginal women; and Baby Jai — Allira's unborn child — were all murdered. Florrie was murdered in Ayr, Queensland. Crystal was murdered in Cairns, Queensland. Allira was murdered in a suburb of Sydney in New South Wales. At the time of her murder, Allira was five months pregnant with Baby Jai, who was also killed.

Florrie, Crystal and Allira were daughters, sisters, aunties, mothers and a grandmother. They were caught in relationships that were difficult to get out of due to the power and control of the perpetrators. These women had different life stories, but they died in similar circumstances — at the hands of their partners or former partners. Their families have given permission for me to include their stories in this book. I am deeply thankful that they have trusted me to share these stories of their loved ones. I've called this chapter 'Know their names' to make the point that their names should never be forgotten.

Florrie Reuben

> I always remember Mum bringing laughter to the family and people that were around her. And, yes, just being a loveable person and that light, I suppose, for everyone that was involved in her life. And especially for me and my little brother. (**Tom, Florrie's son**)

Sis — Florrie — passed in 2022. I call Florrie Sis because her son Tom is a close family friend. Her passing was not long ago. However, the events that unfolded in August 2022 remain unclear for Tom and the family. The person responsible for Florrie's death never went to trial as he died from self-inflicted injuries just as police were preparing to charge him.

Florrie was a proud Peidu and Samsep woman from Erub Island in the Torres Strait and a proud Aboriginal woman from the Gabi Gabi people of K'gari in Queensland. Tom wants people to remember his mum as a woman who gave herself to her family and friends, had a good-natured heart and liked to make people laugh. Tom wants people to remember his mum as she was, not how she passed. He wants her to be known as the beloved mother, sister and grandmother that he and his family knew her to be.

Crystal Ratcliffe

Crystal Ratcliffe was a Kalkadoon woman. She was raised in Gimuy (Cairns), in Far North Queensland, where she lived all her life. She was a loving and caring woman who put family first. She put other people's needs before her own. Crystal loved her children deeply and wanted the best for them.

Crystal's sister, Melissa, talked about what life was like with her younger sister. The care in Melissa's voice when we talked, and the way she honoured Crystal's story, can only be described as a profound sisterly love.

> She was the most loving mother. She was everything about her kids, and family. She used to get away with everything. She was the spoiled

> one and that, and, yeah, when I used to growl, my dad used to stick up for her. So yes, she couldn't do anything wrong. But, yeah, she was a lovely little girl growing up and that. She loved AC/DC, that was her band. When they came to Cairns, she went to the concert and she wore a little tiny top, and she had AC/DC painted on her belly, and there's a video where she was having the best time, because that's my dad's favourite band too, AC/DC. So, she just followed on with him. **(Melissa)**

Allira Green and Baby Jai

> I couldn't tell you how many girls she used to bring home as a kid because they got in trouble off their parents or they've run away from home and she'd bring them all home, you know, I'd ring the parents, tell them they're here ... that's just how she was, she was so giving. **(Nardia, Allira's mother)**

Allira was a Dhungutti woman from New South Wales who had a warm and loving heart and would open her home to others in need. Allira's mother, Nardia, was telling me how, as a teenager, Allira often brought young people home for a warm bed and some food, at which point Allira's brother Lachlan came into the room and joined our conversation. I got the sense that there was a deep brother–sister connection between Lachlan and Allira.

> **Nardia:** I was just saying how your sister was, how she was always bubbly and funny and ...
>
> **Lachlan:** Dramatic ...
>
> **Nardia:** Dramatic ... What else? ... What else do you reckon sissy would've been, Lach? ... She was a bit of a character ...

Lachlan: She used to like [the television series] *Jersey Shore* and all that stuff ... She used to like every music ...

Nardia: Allira loved [the country music duo] Brooks & Dunn, that bloody song, what was it? ...

Lachlan: 'Neon Moon' ...

Nardia: That's her favourite song, and she'd play it constantly... constantly...

Lachlan: Every blackfulla's favourite song ...

Nardia: We got a disco, all her friends and — it was big, hey Lach, sissy's wake, hey? And they all danced to her songs ...

Marlene: 'Neon Moon' must've been on repeat, was it? ...

Nardia: Yes, that was the opening and that was the ending and in between ... Every girl or every [one] of her friends just requested their songs that they had with her ...

While the memories brought laughter and jokes, our discussion was bittersweet. I'm a mother myself, and I have no idea what it must have been like for Nardia to lose her only daughter and then contend with the systemic issues that followed during the judicial process and conviction.

> She'd light up a room with that smile, she'd always make a joke, crack a joke and then it's all open, you know, that's the sort of kid she was, you know? And she was a naughty kid too sometimes because she'd take off and sneak out, you know teenagers, sneak out and come back at one, two o'clock in the morning and I'd be waiting in the back door. Yeah, she gave me some grief at times. But, yeah, she was so bubbly and she was gorgeous. (**Nardia**)

THE EXPERIENCE OF BEING A NON-IDEAL VICTIM

My intent in this book, as I mention throughout, is to present the stories of the women I spoke with and to share their experiences of violence. As such, I do not aim to provide a thorough overview or carefully balanced report of the cases discussed in this chapter, nor to examine the legal background that has led, since colonisation, to the position Indigenous women currently find themselves in when engaging with the Australian court system. As I spoke about in Chapter 2, Indigenous women are often presented as the aggressors or as unreliable witnesses. Suffice to say, both Allira and Crystal were spoken of in ways that misrepresented who they were, illustrated in the trials conducted for their murders.

In the trial concerning Allira's death, the defence team implied that Allira had been the aggressor in the days leading up to the fatal incident and the actions of the accused were those of self-defence. This is corroborated in the court submissions for the offender. But Allira's mum, Nardia, did not agree with this view.

In the trial for Crystal's murder, the defence team presented multiple stereotypical narratives about her, which were then reported in the media — including that Crystal engaged in risk-taking behaviours and associated with 'undesirable' people. But Melissa, Crystal's sister, disagreed with these representations.

In both cases, the defence teams attempted to cast doubt about the characters of the murdered women in ways that suggested they were somehow responsible for or contributed to their own deaths. Based on agreed facts alone, Allira would have been considered a non-ideal victim using Christie's (1986) criteria, as I discussed in earlier chapters of this book.

It may be standard practice for defence teams to promote doubt and argue that their clients are not guilty of the charges presented. The legal right to innocence until proven guilty is an important part of our common law system. However, tactics that present survivors as unreliable witnesses are more pronounced when Indigenous women come forward with charges (Murphy-Oikonen et al. 2022). In Allira's case, she did not survive, yet she was considered an aggressor by the defence team because she fought back. The defence team discussed at length her history of substance use and her participation in activities they classed as immoral, unethical and illegal. These representations are exacerbated by media coverage that both reflect and add to the denigration of Indigenous women.

TRIAL AND MISTRIAL

For Nardia and her family, the trial relating to Allira's death did not come without challenges. The first trial commenced in May 2015. By June 2015, the jury was unable to reach a verdict and was discharged, resulting in a mistrial. A retrial commenced in November 2015. On the second day of the retrial, the prosecution accepted a guilty plea for manslaughter based on excessive self-defence. In New South Wales, a conviction of manslaughter carries a term of up to 25 years in prison. The presiding judge referred to the offender's actions involving a high order of criminality and, in November 2015, the offender was sentenced to 12 years and nine months — comprising nine years and six months of imprisonment, followed by three years and three months on parole. He was due for parole on 2 February 2023, with the balance of his term to conclude on 2 May 2026. However, in an appeal made in April 2016, the offender was resentenced to 12 years, with a non-parole period of nine years, which made him eligible for parole in August 2022. Today, Nardia and her family are not only haunted by the death of Allira, but also by the fact that the convicted person was paroled to an address not far from them.

> You've got to remember we had a mistrial and we had to go again, in the end I just took the manslaughter, I couldn't deal with it any more. Because it was 12-and-a-half [years] ... so it's like how do they justify that? How — It's like your daughter was all at fault, and I

> couldn't be her voice, you know, I just wanted to — there was stuff that [the defence] would say. And you just sit there, and you just listen to all that bullshit, but we're not allowed to say anything in our victim statement on how we're feeling and [what] this person has done to us as a family. They pick and choose — you write it, send it off, the DPP [Director of Public Prosecutions] will send it off to his defence and they say, 'oh, no, you can't put that in there' or 'oh no, we don't want that put in there'. (**Nardia**)

Jai's Law – a proposal for change

At the time she was killed, Allira was approximately five months pregnant with Baby Jai. His death was not recognised as a separate crime; in law it was treated as a consequence of the fatal injury to Allira. The offender was convicted of manslaughter in relation to Allira alone. That outcome reflected the law as it stood in 2013. Although the *Crimes Act 1900* (NSW) has, since 2005, defined grievous bodily harm (GBH) to include 'the destruction (other than in the course of a medical procedure) of the foetus of a pregnant woman, whether or not the woman suffers any other harm (s 4), this definition merely folded the loss of a foetus into harm to the mother. It did not create a separate victim, nor did it allow a standalone charge for the death of Baby Jai.

In late 2021, NSW enacted reforms commonly known as Zoe's Law, creating, for the first time, stand-alone offences where a criminal act causes the loss of a foetus. These reforms inserted s 54A (GBH-based foetal loss) and s 54B (an additional penalty when the pregnant woman is killed and the foetus is also lost) into the *Crimes Act*, commencing 29 March 2022. Both provisions apply only if the foetus is at least 20 weeks' gestation or 400 g in weight (if gestation cannot be reliably established) and they expressly exclude lawful abortion and any act/omission of the pregnant woman (ss 54A(6)-(7); 54B(5)-(6)).

Why this gap matters and what the law should say

Zoe's Law was designed in response to third-party criminal acts (notably dangerous driving) that result in foetal loss. Government publications and media reports emphasised this origin, the 20 weeks/400 g threshold, and the need to protect both abortion law and the pregnant woman's autonomy. But the method of harm — knife, fist, gun or vehicle — does not change the reality of the loss, nor the depth of grief felt by families like Nardia's, who lost two loved ones, Allira and Baby Jai. The law's current structure means that in many family and domestic violence contexts the death of an unborn child may still remain legally invisible unless the timing, gestation and evidentiary requirements neatly align with the new offences. This risks perpetrating precisely the invisibility and devaluation of Indigenous women and their children that this chapter has exposed.

What should change?

The loss of an unborn child is a distinct and profound form of grief — one that touches not only the mother, but the entire family and community. All Australian jurisdictions should extend their criminal laws to recognise this loss wherever and however it occurs, not only when caused by a vehicle or a stranger, but also when caused by someone known as in the instance of intimate partner violence. NSW has taken an important step through Zoe's Law, but this protection remains jurisdiction-specific and is not yet clearly or consistently applied in cases of killings related to domestic and family violence (DFV). Extending similar provisions across Australia — and clarifying their application in DFV contexts — would ensure that when an unborn child such as Baby Jai is lost through violence, that loss is not rendered legally invisible but is recognised as the separate, irreplaceable life that it is, whether the harm arose from a weapon, fist, firearm or car. And while Zoe's law cannot apply retrospectively, a new law — Jai's Law — could ensure that future families, like Nardia's, who experience such tragedies are met with justice that genuinely reflects the full scope of their loss.

COURTROOM THEATRICS

The courtroom serves as the public's window into the tragic reality of murdered Indigenous women and children. For families, though, court proceedings create a space in which legal teams carve out specific narratives — which then become the dominant story reported in the media. Their loved ones' personal lives are displayed before the court and presented in ways that can be distressing or invasive — often purposefully designed to create reasonable doubt in the minds of the jury, prosecution or judge.

Unfortunately, the court environment is often neither culturally supportive nor trauma-informed. I have been present in multiple court sittings, and I believe the environment — with its formal language, procedural complexities and often hostile atmosphere — can itself be a form of violence. It can retraumatise families, compound their grief and create a sense of powerlessness as they hear the arguments put before the court by legal teams.

When domestic violence cases proceed through the courts, the process can be long, complex and deeply traumatic for the families involved. Crystal's sister Melissa and her family endured a five-year legal journey before the court finally sentenced the perpetrator to life in prison for Crystal's murder. That period included significant delays, including a protracted assessment under the *Mental Health Act* after the accused raised psychological issues while incarcerated — an interruption that intensified the family's uncertainty and distress. Melissa described to me the emotional toll of preparing and reading her victim impact statement, an experience that required her to relive the violence and loss in front of a courtroom of strangers. She also spoke of the instant, overwhelming relief she felt when the verdict was finally handed down — a moment that brought not closure, but a measure of validation after years of waiting to be heard.

> That was the best thing I've ever heard for a long time, in five years actually, yeah, because it was like a weight was lifted off. Well, the

> weight wasn't lifted off. The weight was lifted off after I said my piece in court. It was like 80 per cent of me just went, phew, I've done it, and I've got all my people here with me. I'm not by myself. And I feel confident knowing that he's going to go to jail. And then when they said life. What did I do when they said life? I just — yeah, I just clapped. (**Melissa**)

Crime of passion: an old excuse in today's courtrooms

I was an observer in the courtroom during the sentencing at the trial for Crystal's murder. Along with her family, I witnessed firsthand the defence team's attempt to frame the perpetrator's brutal attack within an antiquated and deeply problematic narrative — as a 'crime of passion'. There was nothing loving nor passionate about the way Crystal was murdered, and I wanted to understand the origins of this narrative. I spoke with a legal colleague who confirmed the historical nature of the term, and I was surprised that it was still being used.

The 'crime of passion' narrative is deeply embedded in historical legal frameworks that once excused violence against women (Nourse 1997). The narrative is not a neutral legal or psychological concept but is entwined with historical and patriarchal structures. Its use perpetuates a patriarchal system in which violence is downplayed and femicide is excused. As a courtroom observer, I noticed this language as a tactic of the defence — used to weaponise societal biases and minimise the severity of the crime against Crystal. By framing her murder as a 'crime of passion', the defence team aimed to disregard the documented history of controlling behaviour, jealousy and threat that preceded the tragic event. This narrative helped to minimise the premeditated acts by the accused and exacerbated Melissa's family's pain.

Two other things caught my attention during that day in court. First, the defence team used a conciliatory tone to downplay the actions of the offender and portray him as the victim of overwhelming passion rather than a perpetrator of calculated violence. Second, I noticed a disparity in the length of time each legal team took to provide their closing remarks. The defence spoke for around ten minutes, while the prosecution's remarks took two hours. Perhaps this was the defence's way of conceding that, as the offender had pleaded guilty earlier that year, the sentencing was a simple formality.

The judge's observations stood in stark contrast to the defence team's comments. In sentencing, the judge highlighted the accused's selfishness and his refusal to accept the end of the relationship — behaviours that demonstrated long-term planning and a deliberate disregard for Crystal's choices and autonomy. I felt that the judge recognised the coercive and intentional nature of the accused's actions and made visible who Crystal was to her family, as well as the profound loss they continue to endure.

MEDIA ATTENTION

When fatalities occur, families are often thrust into the media spotlight — perhaps with local news reports or national headlines. Media stories are also shared on social media, with more comments added. Being in the media spotlight can create further trauma for survivors and families. The families of Florrie, Crystal, Allira and Baby Jai are all at different stages of their experiences with the judicial process, and they've all experienced the media spotlight.

The three families talked to me about their experiences with the media — which perpetuated the narrative of the non-ideal victim. In Crystal's case, the journalists covering the trial repeated the language and wording the accused used in court. While this may be perceived as impartial journalism, it caused further harm to Melissa and the family. At times, they were unaware of what had been said until they saw it in the headlines or on social media. The media reports included defamatory allegations about Crystal in a way that removed her voice and her agency. Melissa felt that being thrust into the media spotlight was a violation of her family's privacy that perpetuated an already agonising experience.

> And then they started making up stories about it in the paper, that she was with a bikie gang, and she was doing drugs. And this is what we had to go through over the years, and it's all because of him, what he said in court ... She hated drugs. [And] she's not here to defend herself. (**Melissa**)

During our interview, Florrie's son Tom spoke about seeing pictures and stories of Florrie in the news media and across social media. While he understood that journalists and people posting on social media may have had good intentions, he found it confronting to see the story in newspapers at the local shops or when he went online. He felt the media coverage added to his family's grief.

> I didn't mind, but at the time it was really raw, and we were only just trying to get our heads around what had just happened, and they [media] were just on our case. All the posts and that on Facebook and anything else. And like even going down to the local shop round from where we live, they had a photo — picture of mum in the paper. (**Tom**)

Given Tom's experience with the media and the reporting of Florrie's passing, I asked him what he'd like to say to journalists who report on these stories.

> I'd tell them, from my experience, like, just to leave the family alone and let them go through the process, feel the emotions and sort of try and grasp what had happened. Just let them be until they're comfortable and they're ready to speak. The media should just give families the time, and space, to let them grieve how they want to grieve. (**Tom**)

For Nardia, the media were an impediment to the family's desire to grieve together, in private. The family had to move swiftly, to ensure close family and friends heard the news from Nardia and not online.

> The media were chasing us for weeks. I didn't want to talk to anybody. (**Nardia**)

SYSTEMIC FAILURES TO PROTECT INDIGENOUS WOMEN

As I explore later in this book, I have encountered several troubling examples illustrating systemic failures in responding to violence against Indigenous women. In many cases, response times to complaints were alarmingly slow, or requests for assistance were downgraded — from urgent domestic violence callouts to mere welfare checks — thereby diminishing the perceived severity of the situation. Such examples resonate strongly with the families of women like Florrie and Allira. When I spoke with Tom, he said there was an active protection order in place at the time of the fire that caused the injuries to Florrie. Tom said he couldn't understand why the police did not act to remove the person named on the protection order from the house that they shared with Florrie. Later that morning the police were called back to the house to find Florrie with severe burns to her body requiring immediate attention. Both Tom and I wondered whether a different police response — with the perpetrator being removed — would have saved Florrie's life that night. The police had an opportunity to intervene and apprehend the perpetrator, but they failed to act decisively to protect Florrie.

Similarly, Allira's case highlights a pattern of reluctance by authorities to enact protection orders, even with a documented history of violent callouts and a known history of violence by the perpetrator. Allira's family believe that there was a reluctance to proceed with a protection order that ultimately resulted in her tragic death and that of Baby Jai. Her story illustrates a troubling systemic failure — an inability or unwillingness to prioritise the safety of Indigenous women despite clear warning signs.

Addressing these failures requires a critical examination and deconstruction of how protective measures are applied and a commitment to ensuring these systems genuinely serve to protect Indigenous women instead of undervaluing their safety. Without urgent reform, these tragic outcomes are likely to continue.

CHAPTER 9

MY STORY CONTINUES – SEARCHING FOR A SAFE PLACE

In the early 1990s, I was in my late adolescence. I left high school in 1992, at the end of Year 11. School wasn't for me. I didn't conform and didn't respond well to the way the education system was trying to condition me. Moreover, I felt the system did not support my needs.

I was an awkward and shy teenager — which I now understand stems from my experiences of trauma. I'm still an introvert most of the time. I am awkward when the spotlight is on me and I do not like to be the focus of attention. But as people get to know me, I can become extroverted at times. As I've mentioned in earlier chapters, I had witnessed and experienced various forms of violence. I spent time with family members when they (or we) were escaping episodes of violence. I often carried my younger cousins when we fled violent situations. If we were lucky, we had some clothes in plastic bags. I remember that sometimes we left places with just the clothes we were wearing.

As a teenager, I sometimes lived with my mum, and sometimes with my Nan or my aunties. I had places to stay, but I didn't ever stay in one place for long. As I've already mentioned, these were difficult years for me. I was enduring the aftermath of a rape and dealing with the daily struggles of being an adolescent.

I wasn't one to take risks— at least, I didn't consider myself someone who took risks. When I look back, I realise there were times when I took big risks. One time, I hitchhiked from one side of town to the other. I needed to get from point A to point B, and I'd seen other members of the community hitching rides — I didn't think of it as risky. My mother and her eldest sister would be mortified to know I'd done something they would consider to be an unacceptable risk. But I did it without thinking. Come to think of it, I'm pretty sure one of my mum's cousins drove past me on the road at some point, but they didn't stop to give me a lift.

In Year 9, a few months after I was raped and the attempted suicide, I ran away from home. I mentioned this briefly in Chapter 4, but I want to discuss it in more detail here. This time of my life was weird. I didn't tell anyone what had happened, and no one knew I had attempted suicide. I ran away from home, mostly because I thought I was a burden on my mum.

My mum was a single parent, raising a teenager who had plenty of issues. Mum and our Nan were the main driving forces for my education. Mum worked in the education system. Her family raised me and supported me — they've supported me through my life. When I ran away from home as a teenager, I ended up going to a friend's place in Sydney. I can't remember how I got there — most likely by train. My trauma brain has blocked a lot of memories. Leaving was an impulsive decision. I didn't have any plans. I had no idea where to get money or where I would stay for the long term. I've now realised that removing myself from a space is my frequent response to trauma — although on the flip-side, self-placement could be considered a strength. I tend to remove myself from situations where I feel unsafe or unwanted. Thus, as a teenager, I didn't stay in one place for too long.

The police found me after I ran away from home. I think I may have been at my friend's place for one night before they found me. They took me to a police station in Sydney and, somehow, I got sent back home. I can't remember how the police located me or how I got back home, but I do remember my biological father picking me up and taking me to live with him. My relationship with my biological father has always been strained, and I only stayed with him for about six months. Then I decided to move back home and spent the next year with my aunty, Mum's eldest sister.

I don't remember a lot from that year, and I think I've repressed a lot of memories. In some ways, I'm glad. It was such a horrible year that I don't want to remember it in detail. I know I felt that at times my community wasn't safe for me, and that life was safer if I was on the move. Being on the move meant that my schooling was disrupted. In Year 9, I think I wagged about 90 days. I didn't feel that school was a safe place, and I felt as though I had no one to turn to. My one safe place was my grandmother's home, and I stayed with her when I could. During this, my most troubled year, she cared for me and kept me connected to school. She could tell something wasn't right. She never asked what was wrong, but she looked after me in ways only a grandmother could.

CHAPTER 10

SEEKING JUSTICE AND SUPPORT

Based on anecdotal evidence gathered from conversations with colleagues and the interviews I conducted, a distressing and consistent pattern emerges: Indigenous women continue to experience high levels of violence, resulting in severe injuries and, alarmingly, a disproportionate rate of mortality. Many accounts describe experiences of ongoing abuse, and systemic neglect within institutions that should offer protection. The repetition of these stories underscores that this is not an isolated issue but a deeply rooted social and structural problem that perpetuates harm against Indigenous women. Addressing this crisis requires urgent, targeted interventions that recognise and deconstruct the power imbalances and underlying causes of violence against Indigenous women.

WHY REPORT? – 'IT WAS VERY HARD TO GET ANYWHERE WITH THE POLICE'

The harsh reality for Indigenous women in Australia today is that our womanhood is *denigrated* and *dehumanised,* and our bodies are regarded as *disposable.* These three D's are confronting to name, but they reflect what Indigenous scholars such as Kylie Cripps (2023) have clearly articulated. Violence against Indigenous women is overwhelming. It is not only prevalent today; it is embedded in Australian history. Time and again we see clear demonstrations that society places little regard or value on the lives and bodies of Indigenous women. As noted by Cripps (2023:306), 'these [coronial] cases ... have arguably devalued Indigenous women's lives through their actions and inactions'.

For me, the three D's link back to my thoughts about the duality of Indigenous women — as the binary of hypervisible and invisible — as discussed in the opening chapters to this book. It leaves me wondering which victims are worthy of protection and safety. Jaylah touched on this idea when she described the importance of seeing people where they are, without judgement. She commented that Indigenous women who come forward to report violence not only have to deal with ongoing feelings of being judged, they also must prepare themselves mentally and psychologically for potentially hostile interactions with service providers. Jaylah's quote below is lengthy, but it articulates the way narratives are framed and the importance of responses by service providers. She illustrates why the violence experienced by Indigenous women is complex, especially where they are not considered as ideal victims.

> Why report? When you're not going to be believed and everything from your past is going to be brought up in court to make you out to be mentally unstable or crazy? And [apparently] you were the one that perpetrated or instigated the violent situation, and he just reacted to your irrationality.
>
> Aboriginal women have a lot of barriers to get through to report violence. They've got to get through the fear of the perpetrator, the fear of his family and friends, and then it's this system.
>
> It comes back to how you're perceived to be as an Aboriginal woman. The court process? I can't say that it is supportive, and I can't say that it does protect women, because women are dying.
>
> And it's just the erasure. Erasing of Aboriginal women's bodies, their voices. Well, it's erasing us as humans because we're perceived in a certain way in terms of how we've been constructed by media,

> by white people. How we're supposed to behave, and if you don't fit the box, you're either angry, hostile or you have an attitude issue. It's this construction of how we are seen in society and if we don't live up to that construction, society doesn't know how [to] handle us. [As an Aboriginal woman] I'm supposed to be this way, I'm supposed to look like that, I'm supposed to act like this. I'm supposed to fit this white idealistic model of what a woman is first, and then what an Aboriginal woman is. If you don't fit that story these stereotypes are created. **(Jaylah)**

Police investigation

I asked the women I interviewed about their experiences with service providers and what happened when they asked for help. Their responses varied. Like Jaylah, Tesha stated it was difficult for her, as the perpetrator was a former government employee — and that made things difficult when it came to reporting.

> I tried to [get help], it was very hard to get anywhere with the police. I went into the police station with the kids, and I was really scared, and I saw the DV [domestic violence] specialist there and then the sergeant came, and explained the situation. I was told he was a dangerous man, and they explained the seriousness of it to me and the danger I was in, so they took a violence order and then had me in a safe house, but he didn't take notice of that, he found me and abducted me ...
>
> The police sort of knew him so they just sort of said, 'oh, we'll have a talk to him' or whatever, they never took it seriously. He knew the system and he knew what he could get away with. They locked him up for a bit. But it was like the police had no power because he had the power in a way. The police didn't scare him. **(Tesha)**

Tesha felt that the police did not take her situation and safety seriously. Tesha mentioned one policewoman who was supportive, but who left her role due to burnout.

> I found it hard with the police, I found that they cover a lot up and it sort of had to become ... a really bad situation for them to take it seriously and the detectives to get involved. But the DV specialist was great. That one policewoman was unreal, however she had to leave the job over it. It just depends on who you see on the day. (**Tesha**)

Tesha recognised that the support she received varied — and I'm left wondering how this is even possible from the police, whose sole purpose is to serve and protect the community. Who was protecting Tesha? Why does it, or why should it, matter who is on duty when a crime is reported? Shouldn't every report receive the same level of support or urgency?

Even after she took the matter to court, Tesha's former partner continued to harass and intimidate her.

> I get grief all the time from him, but I don't report it because it's no use, nothing happens, and it just becomes an event number and that's it. (**Tesha**)

Some women I spoke to said they felt supported by the police, but others did not. It seems that women's success in contacting the police depends on the individual police officers responding to the report. This inconsistency makes it even more difficult for Indigenous women to seek support. If a woman feels unsure about how she'll be treated, whether she'll be listened to, or whether the police will help, she's less likely to trust the system.

Jaylah talked about her experiences with the police. She felt that the police failed to provide the support needed, and that the system was unresponsive and those with the mandate to enforce legislation failed to protect her.

> I believe that the police system and the judicial system is designed to protect the perpetrators and get them the easiest outcome. They don't believe women and they sure as hell don't believe Indigenous women. (**Jaylah**)

When Amahle reported her story of rape and being held in a situation where her life was not safe, the police did not believe her. Amahle felt that the perpetrator manipulated the situation by saying they were in a relationship and that the rape was consensual sex.

> When I was getting interviewed by the police, I mentioned about being raped at knife point and saying other things that this person did to me and because he was saying that we'd supposedly been in a long-term relationship the coppers took his word over mine and basically said that I'd been lying about being raped. (**Amahle**)

Cross-border impediments

Although some laws have changed, and we now have recognition of protection orders across all state and territories, variations in legislation can complicate things for Indigenous women who are seeking justice. Jaylah talked about the difficulties she experienced when living in another state, away from a family member who asked for help in a time of violence. It's possible that the response to Jaylah's triple zero call was standard procedure, but it's also possible that cross-border limitations created difficulties. Sometimes a survivor is unable to go to a police station or call the police themselves, particularly if they're being closely monitored by the perpetrator. If they seek help from a family member in a different state, the situation can become difficult.

> A family member was in another state, she rang me to support her in a time where she was beaten very badly. So, when I tried calling triple zero, they basically said they couldn't help me because she needed to

> ring them herself, and she needed to go in to report the violence. She was too scared to do any of that, and because I wasn't close by, I couldn't take her in or call and sit beside her for support. She still hasn't reported this event. It is too traumatic for her. (**Jaylah**)

THE COURTROOM – JUSTICE OR RETRAUMATISATION?

In cases where Indigenous women do report violence and proceed through the court process, the courts can inadvertently facilitate further violence. Tesha's story is an example of this. The court process mirrored the dynamic of coercion and control she had experienced in her relationship. She described a harrowing moment when she felt like she was 'bashing her head against a brick wall':

> When he abducted me, he raped me and then when it went to court, he got rights to cross-examine me — which I thought was wrong, that he could cross-examine me. But yeah, I felt I was fighting to get help, and it was exhausting. (**Tesha**)

The judicial system has the responsibility to ensure that all parties receive appropriate legal representation, especially in sensitive cases of domestic violence and homicide. Given the gravity of these cases, magistrates or judges could intervene and recommend legal representation for both parties presenting in court, thereby reducing retraumatisation and power imbalances. In Tesha's case, for example, the judge could have recommended legal representation for the perpetrator and prevented him from cross-examining Tesha. This intervention could have shielded her from distressing cross-examination, yet it did not happen. Despite winning her case, the process has left ongoing and lasting scars. The direct ability of a defendant to cross-examine a victim-survivor is now restricted in most states and territories.

Similarly, Nardia experienced ongoing pain from witnessing her daughter's case unfold in court. She told me how Allira was dehumanised, referred to solely as 'the victim' and stripped of her dignity amid accusations and dismissive attitudes. Nardia was emotionally devastated when the defence team and the prosecution agreed that Allira was the aggressor, thereby implying that Allira was partly responsible for her own death.

> I made it my thing to be there at every court appearance, every mention, every hearing trying to get justice for my daughter. But we had a mistrial, and when the case finally came to its end, I just took the manslaughter plea — I couldn't deal with it any more. It felt like everyone was blaming her, saying she was at fault, that she caused her own death. It was just so overwhelming. I wanted to be her voice, but it felt like the system was against us. (**Nardia**)

These experiences reveal how the court process often fails Indigenous women and their families in ways that dehumanise them and perpetuate the trauma experienced. Murdered Indigenous women and those who survive violence are spoken about and questioned in ways that blame or dismiss them — and this serves to reinforce attitudes where women are disbelieved and the broader context of violence and marginalisation is ignored. This underscores the urgent need for reforms that make the justice process more trauma-informed, culturally grounded and, ultimately, fair.

The courtroom should be a space for justice; however, it can often function as a site of retraumatisation and systemic disempowerment — particularly for Indigenous women and their families. Addressing these issues requires a serious deconstruction and re-evaluation of court practices, including protective measures against cross-examination, better training for legal professionals and systemic reforms aimed at making courts genuinely safe and responsive to Indigenous people's needs.

CHAPTER 11

COERCIVE CONTROL AND POWER

> Just the disgust of the control he had over me. I was like a sex slave. I tried so hard to please him. I wonder if he was traumatised. I tried to understand how his mind worked, but it's almost like he was a completely different person, and he would constantly change. I suffered from his hand. I was drugged and raped by him and other men. (**Lenna**)

The experiences of Indigenous women in Australia reflect a profound and pervasive system of coercive control, rooted in historical and systemic oppression. As Lenna recounts, her trauma illustrates the brutal reality of gendered violence.

Foucault (1979) posits that power is not simply held by individuals but is embedded in a complex arrangement of social relations and structures. According to Foucault (1979:202), 'power has its principle not so much in a person as in a certain concerted distribution of bodies, surfaces, lights, gazes; in an arrangement whose internal mechanisms produce the relations in which individuals are caught up'. This means that power operates through a system — a machinery — that produces dissymmetry, allowing for and enabling the oppression of one group by another.

In contemporary Australia, this machinery of power is operationalised through mechanisms such as the legal and penal systems. The distribution of power illustrates how Indigenous populations are controlled and monitored, with the state exercising significant authority over Indigenous people's lives. The systemic bias often leads to Indigenous people being seen as aggressors in times of resistance, or as criminals who require constant surveillance — thus perpetuating cycles of violence and alienation.

A THEORY OF COERCIVE CONTROL

Researcher Evan Stark's (2013) pivotal theory of violence provides insights into the dynamics of coercive control, particularly in the context of interpersonal relationships. He shows how power operates through psychological manipulation and the imposition of control, in addition to physical force. This understanding provides insights into the multifaceted nature of power dynamics, especially as they relate to Indigenous women who experience violence.

Stark (2013) posits that coercive control encompasses a range of strategies employed by a perpetrator to dominate and manipulate their partner, a form of control characterised by emotional, psychological and economic tactics that create an environment of fear, perceived dependency and compliance, without the necessity for physical violence. He emphasises that coercive control can be insidious, operating beneath the surface of relationships and often going unrecognised as a form of domestic violence (Stark 2013). Central to Stark's argument is the notion that power can be imposed by individuals and institutions. This insight is particularly relevant for Indigenous women, who face both individual violence and systemic oppression. Institutions such as law enforcement and social services may inadvertently reinforce patterns of coercive control by failing to provide adequate support to Indigenous women who experience violence or by perpetuating stereotypes that undermine their experiences. Indigenous women experiencing violence may find themselves navigating a complex web of power relations that control their behaviour in both personal relationships and interactions with societal structures.

In the experiences of the Indigenous women and families I interviewed for this book, internalised control mechanisms — whether through a partner's coercive tactics or broader societal expectations — led to profound psychological impacts and further entrenched the woman's feelings of powerlessness.

Indigenous women also experience multiple types of oppression that can increase their vulnerability and affect the ways they interact with service systems and society more generally. The women I interviewed described experiences where they were judged or felt their stories were not believed. They also spoke about their choices to not interact with the system.

> When it comes to my community and my family, we're matriarchal, we're very strong women, so we have our own way of doing things, so it's this clash between the patriarchal system of the white Western world and then the matriarchal system. And it's like, well, [the] colonisers' world will overpower us because they're the ones in power. (**Jaylah**)

American writer bell hooks (2014:1) argues that, in the white heterosexual patriarchal system, 'power is commonly equated with domination and control over people or things'. In Australia, control over Indigenous women relates to the overall control and possession of people, resources and land. This connects to white possessive logic, identified by Moreton-Robinson (2015:xi), who describes it as 'a mode of rationalization … underpinned by an excessive desire to invest in reproducing and reaffirming the nation-state's ownership, control, and domination'. This is a neat way of articulating that Australia's mainstream society rationalises the mistreatment of Indigenous women to maintain power and control. The key words in this comment from Moreton-Robinson (2015) are ownership, control and domination — which connect to the Indigenous experience of dispossession of land, displacement onto missions and reserves, and the ongoing warehousing of Indigenous bodies in a variety of state institutions. The nation's ownership, control and domination extend beyond resources to include the ownership of people who are caught up in government systems.

COERCIVE CONTROL IN INTERPERSONAL RELATIONSHIPS

Coercive control is a calculated strategy employed by people who use violence to manipulate and dominate the behaviours of others, often in intimate partner relationships (Stark 2013). Stark (2013:13) describes coercive control as a pattern of behaviour that seeks to dominate a partner through nonphysical tactics such as isolation, intimidation and control over daily life. It extends beyond physical violence and includes psychological, emotional and financial manipulation, and can create a prison-like environment for its victim (Stark 2013). Jaylah described it this way:

> It was like chipping away, chipping away at my self-esteem, at my confidence and I just went into my shell a lot of the times and just didn't want to be noticed. (**Jaylah**)

The perpetrator of coercive control employs various tactics to ensure compliance, including surveillance, emotional manipulation and the imminent threat of repercussions. These undermine the person's autonomy and self-worth and push them into a state of compliance.

> I remember when he started to groom, it was five years into our relationship when everything started to change. I would suffer 12 more years after that. (**Lenna**)

The women I spoke with said they often felt trapped and powerless, and self-doubt affected their ability to seek support or imagine a life beyond the violent relationship.

> I almost threw the towel in. I used to look [out] the window and pray to our old people and loved ones that passed every single day. I would pray that they would protect us. He tried to send me around the twist. (**Lenna**)

> I remember when I first caught him out cheating. The next day I was leaving to attend a block for uni. He tried to use that argument to ... stop me from going. He said if our relationship was important, I'd stay and talk things out. He had this way of creating arguments before I left for uni, or he'd do something that would make me argue with him, and then he would blame or use them against me. (**Jaylah**)

Coercive control can reinforce a violent partner's manipulation and dominance. The violent partner can control the person experiencing violence through isolation from family, friends and other support networks (which ensures that the perpetrator is the central figure in the survivor's life); surveillance (which limits freedom and reinforces dependency on the violent person); psychological manipulation (for example, gaslighting, whereby survivors doubt their perceptions and reality); intimidation and fear (which creates a power imbalance where the person experiencing violence becomes compliant); and controlled autonomy (in which any semblance of autonomy or decision-making granted by the perpetrator is often superficial).

STRATEGIES OF AGENCY AND RESISTANCE

Survivors often face significant challenges when attempting to leave violent relationships. However, realising personal goals and securing external support networks can help to restore power.

> When it came time to contact him about the divorce, he would try and dangle it in front of me. It was difficult, 'cos I had to serve the

> papers. I had to deliver them to him in person. I spoke to my son, who assisted in being the mediator. Because of the violence I experienced, it was risky. I had a protection order in place. So, my son provided the papers to his father and got them signed. (**Jaylah**)

Despite systemic barriers, Indigenous women demonstrate agency and autonomy in resisting coercive control, often using education and work to reclaim autonomy as a way out of the violence.

> He was a very jealous man. I got my degree and then he made it about me big-noting myself. He had this idea I couldn't do better than him or I couldn't earn more money than him. I would tell him that I was doing this for our family. But he had it set in his mind that I thought I was up myself and that I was better than him. He used a lot of other tactics too, like silent treatment ... Even though he would use all that against me, I was able to redirect some of my energy into those things. I didn't let what he said stop me ... I've done several degrees and ... had a successful career, but hidden this violence at the same time. (**Jaylah**)

A GROSS MISUSE OF POLICE POWER – AMAHLE'S STORY

Each state and territory has either criminalised coercive control or is moving towards criminalisation. While society needs to address coercive control, some precautions are needed before providing police with additional powers.

Amahle shared her experience of being physically assaulted by police after experiencing a violent incident with a former partner. By the time the police arrived at the house, the perpetrator had calmed down. But Amahle was still quite agitated and emotional. The responding police officers identified Amahle as the aggressor and took her into custody.

At the time, Amahle had experienced chronic abuse by her partner over several years. The violence in the relationship was already known to police. Her interactions with police were not positive, and Amahle felt the police did not believe her or consider her story.

> One instance for example was [when] I psyched out, the coppers were involved, I assaulted two police, ended up getting dragged to lock-up. When I was getting taken out of the divi [divisional] van and walked through the police station, I got taken out the back to the cells. I was handcuffed, and my shoes were taken off me. They chucked me, eight very big police officers chucked me to the ground, belted the living hell out of me, kicking/punching everything, by the time they'd finished I wasn't very healthy, but anyway, I got pulled back up by handcuffs which broke my wrist to stand there and see a female police officer in all her glory, laughing at the fact that I'd just been flogged by eight blokes. So consequently, I spat at that lady and, like I said in court to the judge, no woman should laugh at another woman copping a flogging, especially off police. That and one other occasion is the reason why I don't hold trust for police. I'd just come from a bad situation of abuse and violence at the time. I was pretty well intoxicated; I'd found out something that someone had said and acted on it inappropriately which led to the situation. I mean, yeah, I know the police had to be called and all the rest of it, but I'm only a little person and I was extremely little back then, eight police officers don't have to bash what was a 48-kilo, five-foot-nothing woman, you know, like that's just being over the top, male dominance as far as I'm concerned. **(Amahle)**

Amahle was charged with assault for spitting on a police officer and was required to attend the local court. She spoke about the ordeal and the injury she sustained from police violence. Amahle said that she felt the female police officer did not provide any support or attempt to intervene, even though Amahle was mistreated by the male police. She believed the police used excessive force.

In these experiences for Amahle, power rested with the police. While there were cross orders (that is, protection orders were in place on both Amahle and her partner), it seems that she was identified as the aggressor. When we spoke, Amahle was upset about the female police officer's inaction and felt the female police officer had laughed at the way she was treated, although the response was possibly embarrassment. For Amahle, the situation represented a gross misuse of power that resulted in an horrific experience and physical injuries. Perhaps Amahle's reaction would have been different if she had felt supported and well-treated in police custody, rather than feeling that her voice was not heard and that her story was invalidated.

Another time when Amahle reported violence to the police, she was again disbelieved. She reported sexual, physical and mental violence, yet the police still did not support her.

> This one time it was a very violent situation, I was sexually violated, I was physically violated, I was mentally violated, yeah, and I thought, yeah, I'll go to the police. Well, the police got called to the situation ... The so-called detectives that were working on my case didn't seem to think that I'd [been] through any of this. I basically walked out with an eight-month suspended sentence for public nuisance because, once again, he [the perpetrator] got believed over me. (**Amahle**)

I asked Amahle to clarify the experience and whether the police believed the sex had been consensual, and she described what had happened. Her partner had held a knife to her throat and forced her to do things she didn't want to. She was in fear of her life.

> On the consensual side, you've got a knife held to your throat and being forced to do something or otherwise you're going to get your head cut off, like seriously? (**Amahle**)

As a result of her interactions with police, Amahle was unable to trust police and said she would not go to them again for help. She feared them because she was physically injured by police and disbelieved when sharing her testimony of violence.

Intersecting factors, resistance and agency

Amahle's interactions with the police and her experiences of violence illustrate the complexities of power dynamics. Patricia Hill Collins's (2002) matrix of domination provides a framework for understanding how forms of oppression intersect. In Amahle's case, race, gender and class contributed to the power dynamics and shaped the responses she received from institutions designed to protect her.

The first aspect is police dominance. The police represent an authoritative institution with power to enforce laws and maintain social order. In Amahle's case, their power became a tool for oppression when she was treated as the aggressor even though she needed to be protected from violence. In failing to support her and in criminalising her behaviour, the police demonstrated how they can misuse their power. Amahle's descriptions of being beaten while restrained and having her wrist broken suggest a profound misuse of authority. She experienced institutional betrayal, where people in a trusted position failed to protect someone who had experienced violence. Instead of receiving support, Amahle faced further violence — an experience common among marginalised groups whose voices and experiences are silenced and ignored.

Another key aspect is the power dynamic that played out. The power relationship between Amahle and her non-Indigenous partner further complicated the situation. Amahle's partner had a criminal history and

Amahle believes he understood how to manipulate the police narrative. This enabled him to maintain control over Amahle and her interactions with the criminal legal system. His manipulation hints at broader systemic issues, where racial and gendered power imbalances come into play.

Amahle's partner maintained a calm demeanour during police encounters, and demonstrated how individuals can leverage institutional biases to their advantage. He was able to present himself as non-threatening, and this allowed him to escape accountability. This underscores how power can shift, based on race and gender dynamics.

> Well, the men didn't get taken [laugh], I got taken. That's it; because I fought back ... and because he was a white man too. The police did [charge me] so that was a whole turnaround [laugh]. (**Amahle**)

Amahle's demographic characteristics intersect to create a unique set of challenges. As an Indigenous woman, she navigates a world constrained by systemic racism, misogyny and ableism. Her injuries, which stem from long-term violence, complicate her situation and force her to address the ongoing impacts of trauma on her health and wellbeing. Amahle experienced childhood violence and ongoing violence from her partner, and her personal history reveals the cumulative effects of trauma. For Amahle, the combination of medical conditions, little institutional support and a perception that she is less credible than her partner because of her race and gender position her as combative or aggressive. The result is that these factors reinforce the cycle of violence she attempted to escape.

Amahle's story, however, reflects a form of resistance. She defended herself against her partner and used violence herself, illustrating 'violent resistance' where those who experience violence fight back in self-defence (Johnson 2008). Her resistance highlights the complexity experienced by Indigenous women, challenging societal narratives that often vilify those who react to violence.

SURVIVOR OR AGGRESSOR? SELF-DEFENCE AND THE SURVIVAL INSTINCT

Indigenous women increasingly face incarceration for crimes such as manslaughter or murder, often because they chose to fight back against the violence in their lives. Indigenous women who defend themselves are frequently misidentified as the aggressors. This complicates their access to protection and justice. Understanding this dynamic is essential, as it exposes systemic failures in the ways that law enforcement systems respond to interpersonal violence.

> When he had me in the kitchen and he was coming at me, I just went to kick him away from me and he goes, 'don't you hit me', and that made him worse. I defended myself, that made him worse. **(Kya)**

Many Indigenous women report that ongoing violence leads them to respond in self-defence. Kya's comment shows that survival is a first instinct—her instinct for survival led to defensive actions intended to protect her from violence. But these defensive actions can be misinterpreted as aggression by first responders such as police. In situations where women have endured violence—as experienced by the women interviewed for this book—a context is established in which the woman's self-defence is easily misconstrued by authorities. When police respond to a domestic violence callout, they are typically responding to an individual call, without the context of the history of violence in the relationship. In these circumstances, the woman may appear to be the aggressor. The very act of fighting back can become a point of criminalisation, misrepresenting what is a survival instinct.

There is a notable absence of literature addressing the misidentification of those who experience violence, as illustrated through Amahle's story. Heather Nancarrow and her colleagues (2020) highlight the challenge of accurately identifying the person most in need of protection and shed light on the complexities experienced by police and court systems in distinguishing between the survivor and the perpetrator. This is particularly pronounced in cases involving Indigenous women.

When the perpetrator manipulates the situation, the identification process is further complicated. Perpetrators might craft a narrative that positions them as the victim, thereby diverting attention away from their violent behaviour and causing confusion for law enforcement and judicial systems. This scenario can also play out in family law matters, where a court determines whether the perpetrator of violence should retain access to children.

The increasing incarceration of Indigenous women for violent responses in the face of violent relationships highlights significant flaws in legal and social support systems (Cripps 2023). The case of Jody Gore in Western Australia is just one example in which an Indigenous woman has been misidentified as the aggressor (Douglas et al. 2020). Despite her pleas of self-defence, Jody was sentenced in 2016 to life imprisonment with a minimum non-parole period of 12 years, after fatally stabbing her former partner during a violent altercation. Although she was eventually pardoned, her case is emblematic of failures within systems that neglect the safety of people who experience violence, particularly Indigenous women.

THE SYSTEM RESPONDS DIFFERENTLY TO DIFFERENT WOMEN

System responses to Indigenous women who are experiencing violence — most notably police responses — reveal significant disparities shaped by factors such as race, gender and socioeconomic status. While some of the women I spoke to shared supportive interactions, others experienced inadequate support and felt they were being judged for their Aboriginality. Some women were left feeling vulnerable and neglected by the system. The women's experiences illustrate the complexities of system responses and emphasise the importance of advocacy and systemic change.

Several women reported police and court encounters characterised by unsupportive attitudes, racial bias and gendered discrimination. Nia recalled a distressing experience with a mediator, which underscores how systemic failures compromised her safety and reinforced existing power dynamics that appeared to favour her former partner.

> When we went for mediation, my ex, he's known to the police, I never reported him for the domestic violence but he's known for it ... so he assaulted my now husband, my daughter and I, we were in my husband's car and my ex was punching the window trying to smash it where my daughter was. The police were called, and [my ex] assaulted a female police officer. Even with all of this, when we went for mediation, the mediators pretty much let him have as much access as whatever he needed. I'd been told by police to move out of the area for my safety, and with mediation, they made it that I had to travel back three times a month so that he could have the weekends with my daughter, and he had her all of the school holidays. I feel like the court really stuffed up there. (**Nia**)

Not all experiences with law enforcement were negative. Malia described an interaction where she felt supported after an attempted kidnapping.

> I only had a little bit of contact with them [police] at the start. They were good when he turned up and tried to kidnap my daughter that night and I called triple zero and had a friend with me, they were there in an instant and searched and searched and they didn't stop until they found him and locked him up and put him away which was awesome. Apart from those ... like back at the initial complaints, back

> at the very start, I didn't have a lot to do with the police themselves; it was mainly just [the] solicitor. The process I didn't find hard. Once you get over that initial fear, it's not a hard process and they do most of it, you've just got to tell them what happened, and they do the rest for you. The violence orders, there's a lot of talk about those things. People say they're just a bit of paper, they're just a waste of time, maybe, I don't know but they seem to be a good deterrent in my case. I feel like without the violence order that it would have been a little bit more tempting for him to do something to one of us. (**Malia**)

Malia received support from an Aboriginal community-controlled organisation, and her positive experience highlights the critical role of Indigenous services in ensuring that Indigenous women are well supported.

Tesha described a challenging police interaction, where she felt abandoned and frustrated with inconsistent support that led to a sense of betrayal.

> I felt let down, that they didn't protect me enough and he did what he could do. [The police,] I didn't find them real supportive, it was like, oh yeah, we know him rah, rah, rah and then there'd be nothing happen, police really let me down I feel. (**Tesha**)

The different experiences reported may be influenced by the ways police identify and respond to perceived victims. The intersection of race and gender may contribute to biases that dictate which survivors receive attention and support, and which emergency callouts receive the highest priority. In Tesha's case, her former partner's familiarity with the police system raised questions about whether this affected the police response and how the police perceived her reports of violence. It is not clear whether Tesha's experience reflects a systemic bias or whether individual police officers self-select the extent of their engagement. Police officers respond in ways they consider appropriate, based on their perceptions of the situation. While experiences varied widely for the women I interviewed, they depend on the unique circumstances of each woman, the context of the callout and any ongoing relationship with the police and their community.

The experiences of Indigenous women suggest the need for systemic change in how law enforcement interacts with survivors of violence. We should not tolerate a system where some women, like Malia, benefit from supportive advocacy services and positive police responses, while others, such as Amahle, Nia and Tesha, experience significant barriers.

CHAPTER 12

NOT OUR CULTURE, NOT OUR WAY OF LIFE

> In terms of society, I think there's an acceptance that it's just the way. Community really needs to change in terms of the way in which they deal with violence and understand that it's not okay. It's not right to be violent. I reckon it's everyone's business and everyone needs to be aware of it. So many people just turn their head. Speak up! If you're going to allow that sort of thing to happen then you're just as bad as the person doing it because, on the other side, there's a poor girl there who needs your help and if you're going to allow him to do it, you're enabling him as much as he's enabling himself. (**Malia**)

I feel conflicted about what to write in this chapter. There are so many issues to unpack when writing about the violence experienced by Indigenous women. I would like to make one message clear: where violence occurs, the perpetrators must be held to account and take responsibility for their actions. This call for perpetrators to take responsibility is supported by the women who share their stories in this book.

> It's not acceptable. No violence is acceptable at the end of the day. It's still amongst us all. It's just no one talks about it, that's the saddest thing. (**Lani**)

> It's not okay — violence in any way, shape or form, lateral violence, domestic violence, family violence is not okay. It has lasting impacts on the individual, to the extended family, to children and then so on out into the community. We want a community that's somewhere our women and kids are safe and happy, and free of harm and violence to grow and to make a healthy community. We want our community to be on a healing journey as a community and say that that's not okay in our community. (**Anika**)

The history of violence against Indigenous women reported in the media and research is lengthy (Moreton-Robinson 2000; Huggins 1995; Smallacombe 2004; Langton 2018; McGlade 2012; Cripps 2023; Ingram 2016; Longbottom 2018, 2020; Carlson et al. 2024). There's also an ongoing perception that Indigenous people are complicit — that we do not advocate or speak up about the situation, or we avert the gaze by focusing on other issues (Mundine 2016; Panahi 2017). This perception is not accurate. Indigenous women are and have been speaking up. However, when Indigenous women do advocate, they are often branded as hostile or angry (Moreton-Robinson 2000; McGlade 2012; Longbottom et al. 2016).

Jaylah and Malia commented on the need to call out violence and ensure those who perpetrate violence are held accountable. Any attempt to demonise or blame the survivor needs to stop.

> When we stand up and we talk about it to our nephews, our cousins, our brothers, our uncles, our fathers, the focus is not on them, it's on [the] woman or she's the one that started it and that type of victim blaming has got to stop. (**Jaylah**)

> Community really needs to change in terms of the way in which they deal with violence and understand that it's not okay. It's not right to be

> violent and if your son is being violent you've got to pull him up, no more of this talk like, 'Oh, my baby wouldn't do that sort of stuff', that's bullshit! You've got to call him out for his behaviour and you've got to make sure he fixes it. That comes back to any of our brothers and uncles and fathers and sons and nephews. If they're doing the wrong thing you've got to pull them up on it. (**Malia**)

The women I interviewed experienced violence from perpetrators of various ethnicities — both Indigenous and non-Indigenous. The Australian Bureau of Statistics does not publish the ethnicity of homicide perpetrators (Australian Bureau of Statistics 2025). But we need to remember that Indigenous men are not the sole perpetrators of violence against Indigenous women. All people who use violence should be held to account and made to take responsibility for the violence they inflict — regardless of ethnicity.

> The violence that I experienced was with both Indigenous and non-Indigenous men. My mum has never been with an Indigenous man. A lot of my family and people I know have not been with Indigenous men, so avoiding the discussion around white men being violent needs to come out. (**Jaylah**)

Malia talked about her experience of receiving backlash from a perpetrator's sister. Malia reported the violence because she knew the perpetrator had a pattern of violence. She described her reporting as a strength and felt that it also helped to keep the perpetrator away from other women.

> Well, my experience, from what happened with me, was his sister, when she said to me, 'oh, see, now he's in jail', like it was my fault because I said something and reported it. He had more victims than me and I wasn't going to let him get any more victims, you know what

> I mean? So, I think that's the strength that I get from my grandmother and through God. That's my advice to anyone else ... don't fall for the sorry, don't fall for it, report it. (Malia)

Jaylah acknowledged the complexity of violence and said she believed the system provided limited protection for Indigenous women. While prison isn't the only option, it provides a time of separation that might be helpful. She suggested that violent partners need an opportunity to learn about the root causes of their violence and address their issues.

> Our women are dying. I don't advocate for locking up our people and our men because they're the fathers in our families, but sometimes they must go away for a spell. Sometimes they must learn from their mistakes. (**Jaylah**)

Keira said that communities need to come together and show support for the issues experienced by Indigenous women. This includes the men in the community.

> I suppose community come together and help tackle this, you know what I mean, working together. Services getting together, putting the word out there that women can access certain services and stuff like that, just coming together and helping to build ... a safer community for our women, talking about it. Women, activists, strong women don't want it no more, fighting, enough's enough. Not just women but men as well are coming together to help tackle domestic violence. (**Keira**)

As a result of colonisation, Indigenous cultural practices have been disrupted. Before colonisation, Indigenous communities had clearly defined processes for social order that also included addressing grievances. While it's important to note that not all communities were without conflict or violence (Galtung 1969, 1990), we need to remember that early descriptions and interpretations of Indigenous communities were recorded through a white lens trained to see aggression and interpret conflict resolution as savagery and violence (Hunter 1993; Hiatt 1996; Langton 1988; Burbank 1994; Innes and Anderson 2015). The distorted views recorded by early writers and the adoption of white patriarchal violence have led some men, Indigenous and non-Indigenous, to mistakenly believe they have a right to control Indigenous women. Indigenous men misinterpret Indigenous cultural practice when they claim their actions are based on cultural customs and attempt to link their actions to an Indigenous process of conflict resolution. This distortion undermines the true principles of restoration and dispute resolution in Indigenous communities and is wholly unacceptable.

Keira asserted that violence is not an intrinsic part of Indigenous culture but a misrepresentation fuelled by substance misuse.

> I think the biggest message that we could send to the non-Indigenous people within our community is that, no, this isn't a way of life for Indigenous people, it's not part of culture any of this violence ... [things said like] Them blackfullas they just get drunk and they bash their women around and then that's what they do and that's their way of life, but it's not, it's not our culture, it's not our way of life. (**Keira**)

Lani commented that a strong collective Indigenous voice is essential to combat stereotypes and misconceptions. As noted, Indigenous people who use violence are not a product of their culture, but the result of disrupted cultural processes.

> So, if we have a strong collective community of Indigenous voices, it's sending a clear message to community and white community, that

> this isn't part of our culture. Our community won't stand for it, it's not okay. And that role modelling for our younger generations, boys and girls coming up, that's not our culture, that's not how we roll. And for us to grow up healthy and strong and our community to thrive, we need to stamp all this stuff out and it's everybody's business. (**Lani**)

The violence that Indigenous women experience today diverges significantly from historical conflict resolution practices — where physical violence was not always the default response to conflict, and individuals may have been exiled or banished instead. Western legal systems have stifled Indigenous traditions and replaced timely cultural responses with lengthy judicial processes that exacerbate tensions. Often, justice is not achieved. Viewing conflict through a Western lens can lead to misunderstandings — particularly when expressions of emotion are misread as aggression. For example, Marcia Langton's (1988) analysis of contemporary Indigenous fighting and swearing reveals nuances often overlooked by non-Indigenous observers. While swearing might be interpreted as violent, it can also be a form of expression that carries no intent to harm: '"Obscenities", like explosives, can be used for peaceful as well as aggressive purposes (though of course they must always be handled with care) ... [They] function not only as insults between antagonists... but also good-natured banter in the context of a formally defined joking relationship." (Langton 1988:8)

Kya discussed a contemporary example of conflict resolution in her family:

> My brother attacked me, because I rang the coppers, he spat at me. The next day my eldest son came home, and I said to him, 'stop right there, I need to tell you something, this is what your uncle did to me last night and you deal with it how you deal with it.' That was men's business now and my son was a man then and he could protect his

> mother, so they dealt with it. I said, 'you never done anything?' He replied ... 'You just need to know that we sorted it out, you don't need to know what happened.' The men's business I'm talking about there was that I shouldn't have to go and confront my brother about his behaviour when I have my three sons who are going to be able to look after me. (**Kya**)

Kya's scenario shows how issues can be addressed within the family to reinforce social order without external intervention. It highlights that, even in urban settings and current times, Indigenous communities maintain traditional conflict resolution practices that respect privacy and maintain the cultural distinctions of 'women's business' and 'men's business'. In some communities and despite the impacts of colonisation, Indigenous peoples continue to employ culturally relevant methods for resolving conflicts and maintaining social cohesion.

THE STOLEN GENERATIONS AND CHILD REMOVAL POLICIES

Several of the women I spoke to reported on the impacts of the Stolen Generations. The multigenerational legacy of the policy of removing children and the subsequent trauma families have experienced continue to impact Indigenous people. It remains a very real experience, including in my own family.

Both my parents are Aboriginal. My biological paternal great-grandmother was removed from western New South Wales to Sydney in the early 1900s — though the details of her removal are scant and there are very few records. Her name was changed twice, and her Indigeneity hidden and denied. Her children and subsequent grandchildren, including my biological father, were raised to believe they were 'Australian', and did not identify as Aboriginal. I remember what my great-grandmother looked like, as I saw her on a visit to Sydney when I was around five. I was raised in my mother's family, who are Aboriginal, and I connected with my paternal great-grandmother on another level. Despite the denial and hidden secret of her Indigeneity, I knew who she was and her background — I recognised that she was Aboriginal. Sure enough, in recent times the family history has been explored, and details have emerged that my paternal great-grandmother was indeed a member of the Stolen Generations.

In my mother's family, neither my mother nor her siblings were removed. However, this did not lessen the hypervigilance they experienced. They were always on the alert, and this had a massive impact on my mother and her youngest sister. I've been told by both my mother and aunt, who is the youngest of the family, that as children they were often the focus of welfare workers and, more particularly, the mission manager. My mum and aunt were always being watched. When my grandparents went to work, my mother went with Nan and was hidden under her dress, while my aunt went with my grandfather who hid her under the nets in the fishing boat. My mother remembers that if an unknown car came onto the mission, people would sing out 'cooee', a code to alert the children to hide from the welfare.

Malia described a moment in her father's life when he was told that he had brothers and other family members whom he knew nothing about. Stories like this are common in Aboriginal communities.

> Link-Up[2] phoned my dad and said, 'are you such and such?' And he's like, 'yeah'... And they said, 'oh, we're just phoning up your brother, he's going through a bit of stuff at the moment, and we need to look for kinship care for his two kids.' And my dad's [replied], 'oh, no, sorry mate, I haven't got a brother, I've just got my sister.' And ... they're, like, 'oh, wait, you're blah, blah, blah', and went through all

2 Link-Up is an Aboriginal-run service that helps Stolen Generations survivors trace family, reconnect and heal.

> these details and my dad's, like, 'yeah, that's me ... are you telling me I've got a brother?' And the person went, 'ah, we'll call you back', and then after seven months we've finally gotten some details that my dad didn't just have a brother, he had eight more [laugh] brothers and sisters, so he was one of nine. (**Malia**)

Malia told me what she knew about the moment her father was removed. It is interesting to note the use of Indigenous people in the removal of children. As you'll see, Malia mentions that a tracker was used to locate her dad and her grandmother — this could be considered as similar to using Native Police.

> By [the time of the family reunion], his mum had already passed away, but my dad had actually met his mum accidentally, yeah, and his two best friends through high school were his first cousins. So, his mum, she'd had one baby before him, but that baby was raised by her parents so that he wouldn't get removed and then she got pregnant with my dad and she'd been told that they were going to take him, and she went out bush and they used a tracker to find her. As soon as she gave birth, they took my dad and she went back home and her sister said to her, 'where's the baby?' And she said, 'there is no baby, don't ever talk to me about it.' So no one ever spoke about it. (**Malia**)

As a member of the Stolen Generations, Kima talked about her memories of being removed as a four-year-old and the violence she experienced from the age of six.

> My violence started as a child just from being taken [which] was violence and then to be made white, taught how to talk, taught how to act, taught how to not be black and that brainwashing every single day and the beating every single day. (**Kima**)

PART C

The Journey Beyond Violence

CHAPTER 13

RESTORING POWER — AND A CALL TO ACTION

If I am completely honest, I'm not sure violence in general can be eliminated. Each year, women and children are killed in Australia due to violence. This does not discount the loss of life or the tragedies that unfold; I am simply being realistic. For some women, particularly white women, their tragic stories permeate our consciousness through media reports. While policymakers and advocates set ambitious goals, we must recognise that conflict is inherently part of human nature.

Is this the realist in me? Is it giving up? It's difficult to shake the belief that disputes and conflict will persist. It is a systemic, widespread issue that feels too vast to eliminate completely.

However, even if eliminating violence is not possible, I will always advocate for efforts to reduce its level, severity and type. Most particularly, I advocate for efforts to end the senseless killing of Indigenous women. We need to lift Indigenous women's voices and ensure they are heard. We need to advocate for the agency of Indigenous women and communities. Our cultural practices hold the key to addressing the epidemic of violence against Indigenous women. We need men in our communities, Indigenous and non-Indigenous, to own their behaviours and make a change to ensure the safety of our people. We also need community members to be something more than passive bystanders — we need to hold family and friends to account when they are violent. We, as a collective, need to address this issue. It's not an issue for survivors and advocates alone. We must be unified in making sure that violence is not seen as acceptable or appropriate.

I believe we must challenge Western inscriptions that suggest Indigenous people tolerate or accept violence in their communities. We must accept that our governing practices, which existed for thousands of years prior to invasion, have been disrupted. They remain in only some of our communities — disrupted by the Western way of doing.

As the stories in previous chapters have revealed, the Western legal system struggles to adequately support our women — rather, it often exacerbates their suffering. When a death occurs, our communities are left to grapple with a void. Engaging with the criminal legal system tends to make this worse. Children may be left with one parent who has passed and a surviving parent who is incarcerated. This increases the likelihood of children encountering child protection agencies and potentially being removed from their families. This creates a cycle of violence, system involvement and further violence — a cycle that affects individuals, families and communities. It links to complex interactions with broader systems, including the criminal legal system and the civil and family courts. For many Indigenous women, experiencing violence is just the tip of the iceberg.

ADDRESSING VIOLENCE

The women in these pages — and the families who endure profound loss — have already told us what safety looks like: culturally grounded, community-controlled responses, practical help that restores power day-to-day and systems that stop compounding harm. Their messages are not abstract. They speak of inaccessible courtrooms, child protection encounters that fracture kinship networks and years of living on high alert. Their testimonies insist that change be felt in homes, clinics, courts and community spaces, not only in policy documents.

Into this landscape, the Australian Government released *Our Ways – Strong Ways – Our Voices: National Aboriginal and Torres Strait Islander Plan to End Family, Domestic and Sexual Violence 2026–2036*. It is the first stand-alone national plan dedicated to Aboriginal and Torres Strait Islander women and children; it pledges community-controlled leadership, shared decision making and alignment with Closing the Gap Target 13, which aims to reduce family violence to zero. This plan sits alongside these voices — it does not replace them — and its legitimacy will rest on whether governments implement its commitments in ways that communities can recognise and measure in their daily lives.

I remain cautious with government promises, regardless of how well intended they may be. Funerals of murdered Indigenous women continue, and nothing in a policy document can soften that reality. Communities are left to pick up the pieces, and families like those in this book often become the support network for others, carrying the burdens they never asked for. While I recognise the significance of the stand-alone action plan and its stated commitments to community-controlled leadership and whole-of-system change, I also recognise that the responsibility for transforming systems cannot be placed on Indigenous communities alone. Communities can lead solutions, speak truth, and hold cultural authority — but they cannot dismantle the systemic and structural barriers that have been documented throughout this book. Systems require reform. Only systems can transform themselves.

That responsibility must sit squarely with governments and the institutions that have historically failed Indigenous women, not with a community-controlled sector that is already overstretched and under-resourced. It will be up to the Domestic, Family and Sexual Violence Commission to ensure that these plans do more than name intentions — that they actually move systems, compel accountability and translate promises into real shifts across justice, health, housing, education and child protection. Indigenous communities should never be expected to carry the burden of changing the very systems that have harmed them. Our voices, including those of the women and families in this book, can guide the path, but it is the systems that must look within and do the work to transform.

We need agile interventions that prioritise and build self-efficacy rather than reinforcing binaries of victim/perpetrator or ideal victim/non-ideal victim. While Indigenous women have always possessed strength, their agency and autonomy have been and remain undermined. Fostering self-efficacy is a purposeful endeavour that seeks to rebuild what has been stripped away — for Indigenous women experiencing violence, this can encompass their entire livelihood. This is where we require the restoration of power, not empowerment — as some may suggest.

Violence manifests in intersecting typologies, methods and contexts specific to individual relationships. As people progress through life, both relationships and the enactment of violence evolve. Therefore, adopting a systems approach to providing support is essential, as Indigenous women often interact with systems and services over which they have little control.

To conceptualise this, I draw on the systems approach developed by psychologist Urie Bronfenbrenner (1994). His model provides a theoretical framework for understanding human development and illustrates the ripple effects of violence and the comprehensive efforts needed to provide support. The systems approach can be used to understand key factors that contribute to the complexity of violence against Indigenous women and emphasises the need for agile responses that can be mobilised right across the continuum of care — not only in times of crisis. It can inform choices about how to implement effective support in a way that acknowledges the intricate interplay of individual, family, community and society. The model helps us to understand that violence against Indigenous women is not isolated or episodic. Instead, it is a continuous process of issues that impact different levels of the lives of Indigenous women.

Support and interventions must restore power to Indigenous women and move away from a victim-centric perspective that can render them helpless. To this end, I draw inspiration from the Queensland Indigenous Family Violence Legal Service, which offers a robust framework for assisting Indigenous women and children facing violence and sexual assault, as well as families engaged with the child protection system. The approach by the legal service emphasises the restoration of agency and autonomy by acknowledging the unique cultural and community contexts of Indigenous women. By focusing on agency and self-efficacy, rather than victimisation, this model seeks to create sustainable pathways for healing within Indigenous communities. By leveraging these insights, we can develop solutions that address the complex interplay of individual, community and systemic factors, and provide comprehensive and culturally sensitive support to those affected by violence.

ONE MODEL RESTORING POWER TO INDIGENOUS WOMEN IN QUEENSLAND

A self-determining approach fosters self-efficacy and agency and restores power to women who have experienced violence. It enables them to navigate support systems and care for their families when it is safe to do so.

Self-determination carries multiple meanings. It must begin at the individual level, emphasising agency, autonomy, relatedness and competence. It should lead to self-efficacy (Nakata 2024; Deci and Ryan 2012; Nakata and Nakata 2022; TallBear 2019). This approach transcends strengths-based and trauma-informed practices. It draws inspiration from work on enhancing agency in higher education through self-determination (Nakata and Nakata 2022). Implementing this approach involves adopting Martin Nakata's vision of reconstituting Indigenous self-determination and agency to determine their own futures (Nakata 2024; Nakata and Nakata 2022). This is crucial for maintaining women's agency and autonomy and avoiding the victim narrative that often ensnares Indigenous women.

As part of my research for this book, in 2024 I interviewed two staff members from the Queensland Indigenous Family Violence Legal Service (QIFVLS), an Aboriginal and Torres Strait Islander community-controlled organisation: Wynetta Dewis, the Chief Executive Officer, and Thelma Schwartz, the Principal Legal Officer. We discussed their service delivery framework and the ethos.

QIFVLS exemplifies the self-determining model described above by offering legal services alongside non-therapeutic case management. It complies with Australian law while providing culturally responsive care that focuses on women's self-efficacy rather than dependency. The service model includes a triage process that assesses eligibility for legal representation, case planning, goal-setting and referrals to other services (such as health care).

> So, when a woman may present with a DV [domestic violence] issue ... they'll come in, there'll be an intake, and then they'll get assessed for their legal matter ... and depending then on what level of support that they need, the case management officer will either work more intensively or not. And it's around ... self-efficacy. If the [case management officer] can see that the woman is confident enough to sort of take control of their life ... you've got to just give them A, B, C and they'll be able to follow it, then we just do a touch-base type of support. But if you've got ones who need a lot more support, we'll be there to provide that. So, we do that as an ongoing process along with the legal manager. (Thelma Schwartz, QIFVLS)

The commitment to self-efficacy and capability development allows women to achieve progress gradually and supports them through milestones like gaining independent housing or further education. The service also advocates with the child protection system and provides women with continued support for reunification efforts.

By embedding self-determination theory into practice, QIFVLS helps women to rebuild their agency, autonomy and competency — particularly where they had limited control in relationships that included violence. This culturally responsive approach restores power to Indigenous women in a way that is aligned with their community and cultural contexts.

The service also focuses on connecting women with additional resources through effective referrals, tailored to each woman's needs and circumstances.

> If there's a doctor's appointment, we provide a warm referral, ensuring they are supported to attend ... While we may assist them in getting there, our goal is to build their self-efficacy, fostering independence rather than reliance on us. (Wynetta Dewis, QIFVLS)

QIFVLS adopts a trauma-informed and culturally responsive lens. All staff are aware of each woman's unique history and aspirations. This means that women are not asked to repeatedly share their stories, thus significantly reducing the risk of retraumatisation. The service operates with integrated support internally and collaborates with external agencies and organisations involved in each woman's case. This holistic approach promotes continuity of care and restores power to women on their paths to recovery.

> Making sure that with any of the court work or the legal side of it, we're there to ensure they make their appointments. The case management officer is also helping to break down any of the legal jargon. They'll then be with them in court ... If it's child safety, it's assisting our client to meet any of the child safety requirements. (Wynetta Dewis, QIFVLS)

The QIFVLS approach integrates Western legal practices with case management grounded in Indigenous ways of being, doing and knowing. At the heart of this cultural approach is a case management officer, who serves as a crucial link between the legal team and the client. The case management officer ensures that clients receive emotional and cultural support plus the information they need to make informed decisions about legal matters.

The QIFVLS approach provides comprehensive scaffolding to support women and their families, ensuring a coordinated and tailored response, and staff strive to restore power when women encounter systems such as child protection:

> [I]f the client achieved their case plan goals — dealing with addictions, independent housing, or enrolling in TAFE [Technical and Further Education] — we continue to work with them to achieve reunification, fostering positive momentum. (Thelma Schwartz, QIFVLS)

Small wins are recognised as significant steps toward larger goals. This is particularly crucial for women who have experienced a loss of control in violent relationships or through system mandates such as child protection.

From the perspective of self-determination theory, QIFVLS facilitates women's agency and autonomy through milestones and case plans. The ability for clients to relate to their case managers is key to fostering strong rapport and trust. Competence is reflected in clients' accomplishments, empowering them to progress while receiving ongoing support. This comprehensive approach aids personal development and builds self-efficacy.

The criminal legal system

Building self-efficacy and capability includes fostering a critical awareness of the adversarial nature of the criminal legal system. When seeking court orders related to violence, women face challenges as they navigate legal processes and encounter complexities linked to family law and child protection, particularly if they have previously had their stories disbelieved or if they have been involved with individuals in positions of power within their communities:

> [W]e're building their self-efficacy by addressing non-legal supports ... but when you come into court, it's not a safe space for a victim-survivor. You need to know what to expect ... given the lack of consistency with trauma-informed and culturally meaning training afforded to magistrates, judges and court staff, including lawyers, as it relates to Indigenous women engaging with the court systems. You've got to prepare for the worst-case scenario ... You're going into battle because that's the nature of the system. (Thelma Schwartz, QIFVLS)

QIFVLS prepares clients for negative experiences, recognising that not all judges are supportive. The reality within the legal system can feel overwhelming, and clients often feel marginalised because the criminal legal framework prioritises the defendant's rights, which can be disheartening and can lead to disengagement. The adversarial environment compounds the challenges Indigenous women face and underscores the importance of providing comprehensive support that prepares them for the realities of engaging with the criminal legal system.

> I can understand when they say, 'Look, I don't really want to do this. I'm not ready for it' ... the system is not broken; it's designed to disempower and imprison those who are disadvantaged ... If you don't fit in, the system will pinpoint you, and you will circulate through it. (Thelma Schwartz, QIFVLS)

Significant changes to the legal system have been minimal since colonisation, and Indigenous communities need to draw from their cultural knowledge and practices to inform contemporary approaches. The QIFVLS model illustrates how Indigenous cultural processes can work with legal frameworks — though this requires a shift in the attitude of many within the legal system and efforts to establish genuine partnership. QIFVLS focuses on finding the 'point where you can influence and reset' the system (Thelma Schwartz, QIFVLS), emphasising a proactive approach rather than a decolonising approach (Nakata 2024).

One barrier to consistent progress is the need for high-level champions who can challenge accepted norms. Thelma related a story about a now-retired magistrate who exemplifies the merging of Western legal structures and Indigenous cultural processes. The magistrate engaged with communities, incorporated feedback into the judicial approach and demonstrated the potential for positive outcomes. However, the frequent rotation of magistrates on the circuit court strains the establishment of sustained partnerships and community connections. That this one magistrate chose to take the actions he did, shows that change is possible.

The QIFVLS model is a good example of a practical approach that integrates Indigenous knowledges and practices within the legal framework, creates a more supportive environment for women navigating violence and ultimately leads to the restoration of power. A key strength of the model lies in the central role of case management officers who serve as cultural conduits to bridge the gap between clients and the legal system. They also facilitate connections to support services and ensure the Indigenous community-controlled response is coordinated by Indigenous people and not imposed by external systems.

> We understand that it's not a comfortable situation. You've got to consider immediate needs — housing, food — while being in front of the judge. (Wynetta Dewis, QIFVLS)

THE REPORTING ENVIRONMENT — FEELING SAFE TO SPEAK

In discussions about trauma-informed and culturally responsive services, there is often an expectation that providers will effectively meet the needs of those they serve. However, my research and experiences suggest that many services claim to be culturally and trauma-informed while inadvertently causing trauma or retraumatising the individuals who are seeking help. As the women's stories in this book reveal, the implementation of trauma-informed practices varies significantly. This is where false equivalence does its quiet work: services present the same trauma-informed script to everyone and call it fairness, even though Indigenous women do not enter reporting environments on equal ground.

A critical observation is that Indigenous women who report violence often carry negative past experiences with law enforcement. Reporting violence in environments like police stations can be triggering. When I have visited police stations, I have always found them to be unwelcoming and uncomfortable for discussing personal trauma. Both the police environment and the individuals receiving women's disclosures can contribute to feelings of unsafety and insecurity and create the potential for retraumatisation. It is essential that interviews and disclosure documentation occur in supportive environments that are confidential and help individuals to feel comfortable. This often means avoiding traditional settings such as police stations in favour of more inviting spaces, particularly those within the Aboriginal community-controlled sector.

Some may argue that the small size of Indigenous communities can lead to breaches of confidentiality due to personal connections — particularly if interviews are conducted in these settings. My response is straightforward: reporting needs to happen in a way that prioritises the individual's comfort by finding alternative spaces or organisations. Ensuring that individuals feel safe enough to share their experiences openly and without judgement is key. This fundamental principle recognises that the surrounding environment and the individuals involved can either trigger negative emotions like shame and fear or promote comfort and trust.

Creating a responsive environment is not complex. It begins at the cultural interface: listening first, then allow them to determine where, when and how they feel safe to speak about their experiences. When services adapt their conditions—rather than requiring the women to adapt to the service—trauma-informed care becomes believable and effective.

Yarning and establishing rapport

As a former Aboriginal Health Worker, I have found that some of my most meaningful conversations occur when women are in comfortable settings. These moments often happen during transport to appointments, while sharing a meal or even during activities like fishing. Transportation — when it can be provided — can create opportunities for spontaneous conversations that are simultaneously brief interventions and social engagement.

The nature of these conversations largely depends on what the individual is willing to share and the intent behind the conversation. Spending time together in the car can facilitate relaxed discussions and help to establish trust, especially when people meet for the first time. Similarly, fishing trips, art groups or sharing lunch can create an informal atmosphere that removes the tension often associated with clinical interactions and transforms the yarn into both a social and therapeutic process and has been validated as a research method that privileges Indigenous voices and relationships (Bessarab and Ng'andu 2010).

Yarning is an important platform for discussing experiences that may not necessarily lead to formal reporting. However, yarning is not without its risks to the client or children. In many cases, yarning is less about clinical outcomes than about creating a genuine connection and acknowledging that the women have faced trauma. Even in this setting, though, recounting their stories can be harrowing for women.

It's always important to ensure confidentiality, and sometimes this means organisations need closed-off areas for sensitive discussions. However, it's essential to offer flexibility. A police officer does not always have to receive a statement at the police station. Ultimately, providing opportunities for women to share their stories not only opens a pathway to healing but also fosters a supportive environment that encourages recovery.

THE IMPORTANCE OF FIRST RESPONDERS

Many of the women I interviewed for this book expressed reluctance to report violent incidents to the police. In Indigenous communities, families are often the first responders and provide initial support to women experiencing violence. As I discuss in Chapter 5, in my own family's case, for example, Bud and I banded together to support Kirsty without involving law enforcement, and we were all in different locations. Family-first responses often offer a place to stay — perhaps for a few nights or for the longer term. Families and community networks create an unofficial support system that is often overlooked by formal service providers. Although many families may not recognise the importance of their efforts, they play a crucial role in providing safe havens for women and children.

However, there is a risk in accepting families as first responders and providers of support. Family members who open their homes to support women often become the targets of the perpetrator's violence. They may risk their own safety by helping to ensure the safety of others. Recognising the vital role of first responders in Indigenous communities is essential for creating effective support systems that prioritise safety and agency for women experiencing violence.

Unfortunately, service systems often react to violence only when medical intervention is needed or when third parties, such as neighbours or bystanders, involve the police. Legal protections, such as protection orders against the perpetrator, may also come with counter-orders. Indigenous women often experience delayed or insufficient responses from emergency services, further complicating their situations.

REFLECTING ON MY STORY

As I celebrated my fiftieth birthday in 2025, I found myself reflecting on experiences and challenges I have navigated so far in my life. My journey has involved continuous learning and growth, and I always strive to honour the promise I made to my grandmother by living with integrity and credibility. One significant lesson I learned is that there is indeed life after violence. This truth has been modelled for me by family members, the women and families who contributed to this book, and the inspiring Mrs Sekai Holland (the former Zimbabwean politician I mentioned in Chapter 1).

These days, I am much more at ease with the world — though I still occasionally respond to situations with what you might call dysregulation. Fortunately, these moments are becoming less frequent, as I have made some necessary changes in my life. I continue to manage anxiety and post-traumatic stress disorder. I have sought therapy, I follow a medication regime and I've adopted a healthier lifestyle with good nutrition and regular physical activity. I have also learned to recognise the signs when I am overstimulated and need to take time away from social interactions. This is an ongoing process that remains a valuable learning journey — not only for myself, but also for my son and our extended family network.

As a kinship carer, I have welcomed more children into my home and created a tight-knit family that includes friends and extended relatives who often visit our home. We live together in a four-bedroom house, and I wouldn't have it any other way. Our home is a haven that we've named Bidiga's Place — reflecting on my role as Bidiga, or grandmother in the Dharawal language. The space has emerged from my own experiences with trauma and has transformed my home into a welcoming environment for young people who need care and protection. This space replicates my mum's big sister's home and that of our grandparents. I have created the space that I needed when I was younger, and I believe I've turned into the person I needed at the age when I experienced adversity.

At Bidiga's Place, there is always a bed, nutritious food and plenty of love and laughter. Many weekends I find young people sleeping in my lounge room, which reminds me of my childhood experiences at my aunty's home. Sundays are especially cherished, as I prepare a family dinner and bring everyone together to share stories, reflect on the past week and plan for the week ahead.

In 2025 I graduated with a Master of Social Work — a qualification I pursued out of personal desire rather than necessity. This degree complements my extensive academic background, which now includes a Bachelor of Health Science, three Graduate Certificates, a Master of Philosophy and a Doctor of Philosophy. I have decided to return to study one last time, this time, as a law student, completing a Juris Doctor.

I owe deep gratitude to the women who contributed their stories to this book. The families who shared their stories with me are in regular contact, and we co-present at conferences so they have a platform to voice their lived experiences. I prioritise holding space for these families and hope to write material with them as acknowledged co-authors.

MORE THAN A READER: BECOMING PART OF THE SOLUTION

This book has been a labour of love, a commitment to truth-telling and a testament to the enduring strength of Indigenous women. I have tried to illuminate the often-invisible infrastructure of violence that disproportionately impacts Indigenous women in Australia, and to move beyond simplistic narratives that focus solely on individual incidents. I have also sought to achieve specific goals in:

- **exposing the systemic nature of violence:** I have tried to challenge the pervasive myth that violence against Indigenous women is merely a series of isolated incidents — instead, I reveal the deeply entrenched systemic factors that perpetuate violence, including historical injustices, ongoing discrimination and institutional failures

- **highlighting the legacy of colonisation:** I underscore the historical and ongoing role of colonisation, white supremacy and patriarchal structures in creating and maintaining the material conditions in which violence against Indigenous women can thrive, including examining the ways these forces disrupted Indigenous culture, dispossessed communities of their lands and resources and imposed harmful stereotypes and social norms
- **centring Indigenous voices and experiences:** amplifying the voices and experiences of Indigenous women in a way that recognises their inherent strength, agency, resilience and resistance in the face of adversity has meant creating a space for Indigenous women and families to share their stories in their own words, on their own terms, and without judgement
- **offering an intersectional framework:** I have worked to provide a nuanced framework for understanding the complexities of Indigenous women's lives that acknowledges the multiple intersecting factors that contribute to their vulnerability to violence
- **showcasing culturally responsive approaches:** I have highlighted the importance of culturally responsive approaches to support healing — approaches that emphasise self-determination and community-led solutions grounded in Indigenous knowledge, values and practices
- **restoring power and agency:** I have challenged the dominant narratives that often portray Indigenous women as victims or as tolerant of violence, and I restore their power to define their own narratives, reclaim their voices and advocate for their communities, which includes recognising their inherent strength, agency, autonomy and capacity for self-determination and self-efficacy.

The journey through these pages has been difficult, confronting and, at times, deeply painful. It has required me to confront my own experiences with violence, grapple with the complexities of intergenerational trauma and bear witness to the suffering of others. Yet it is my sincere hope that it has been empowering, inspiring and transformative — not only for me but also you, the reader.

Insights from the First Response Project

After I completed my PhD research, I collaborated with colleagues and four Aboriginal community-controlled health organisations in New South Wales on the First Response Project, which aimed to identify alternative locations for Indigenous women to access support when they experience violence (Lowitja Institute 2019). The project's findings corroborated the learnings from my PhD research.

The First Response Project highlighted that police stations were not always safe places for Indigenous women to report violence. Instead, Indigenous organisations emerged as preferred sites for seeking support. We found that the community-controlled sector was typically trauma responsive and culturally responsive, with soft entry points and holistic service delivery that helped to address women's diverse needs. We also found that the centres benefited from employing both Indigenous and non-Indigenous staff in a variety of roles across safety planning, social and emotional health, physical health and supporting children. For example, when attending a health centre, a doctor can offer crucial support for a woman who is planning to leave a violent relationship. Confidentiality between the woman and her doctor can facilitate safety planning and ensure her protection as she prepares to leave. The doctor can refer the woman to other support staff in the health centre, always ensuring that confidentiality protocols are strictly followed. If the perpetrator's family or friends work in the service, a 'need-to-know' policy can be enforced to prevent breaches of confidentiality. Various staff members can play a vital role in safety planning and the process of leaving, operationalised through training and support from domestic and family violence specialist services, and specialist services can provide guidance on developing policies and procedures.

In Indigenous communities, first responders are not always the police. Therefore, it is crucial for community members to be aware of available services and how to effectively support a woman in crisis. By equipping them with the knowledge and resources necessary to offer support, we can help to ensure the safety and wellbeing of women during critical moments.

WHAT NOW? A CALL TO ACTION

This book is a catalyst, not a conclusion. It is a call to action, a summons to all who envision a future of justice and equity for Indigenous women in Australia. The time for passive observation is over; the time for active participation has arrived. I implore you, the reader, to embrace seven commitments.

- **Listen and believe:** centre the voices and lived experiences of Indigenous women in every conversation surrounding violence, justice and healing. Actively challenge your own biases and preconceived notions, and the ingrained societal narratives that often silence or marginalise Indigenous perspectives. Recognise that their stories are not just anecdotes but vital truths that must inform our understanding and guide our actions.
- **Educate yourself:** commit to a lifelong journey of learning about the complex history of colonisation, the enduring impacts of systemic oppression and the rich tapestry of cultures and experiences within Indigenous communities. Seek out resources created by Indigenous scholars, activists and community leaders to deepen your understanding and challenge your own assumptions.
- **Advocate for systemic change:** become a vocal advocate for

policies and initiatives that address the root causes of violence against Indigenous women. This includes supporting measures that combat poverty, improve access to safe and affordable housing, ensure equitable educational opportunities, provide culturally appropriate healthcare and reform the child protection and criminal legal systems to prioritise family preservation and Indigenous self-determination.

- **Use your platform to amplify not speak over or for:** this is a crucial commitment. You have access to specific platforms, in whatever walks of life you are in. Cede your privilege and provide a platform to amplify Indigenous stories and voices. Do not speak over, or for. We can speak for ourselves. Do not assume that your willingness is allyship and that you are supporting the cause. This action is a fine line. Work with Indigenous organisations and advocates to understand the most appropriate ways to discuss issues that relate to Indigenous women and communities. Be aware that sharing information on social media can sometimes cause more harm than good. Understand the difference between speaking over and for!
- **Support Indigenous-led solutions:** invest your time, resources and energy in amplifying the work of Indigenous-led organisations and grassroots initiatives that are working on the front lines to prevent violence, heal trauma and promote self-determination in our communities. Recognise that these organisations are best positioned to develop and implement solutions that are culturally responsive, community-driven and sustainable.
- **Challenge complicity and disrupt harmful systems:** critically examine your own role in perpetuating systems of oppression, both consciously and unconsciously, and actively work to dismantle them. This includes challenging racism, sexism and other forms of discrimination in your personal relationships,

professional setting and the broader community. Be willing to disrupt harmful systems, even when it is uncomfortable and inconvenient for you.

- **Demand accountability:** hold perpetrators of violence accountable for their actions, and demand accountability from institutions that fail to protect Indigenous women. This includes advocating for reforms to the criminal legal system, supporting restorative justice initiatives and challenging the systemic biases that often lead to disbelieving or dismissing Indigenous women's experiences.

LOOKING AHEAD: A FUTURE FORGED IN DEFIANCE AND HOPE

I see hope on the horizon. Conversations are emerging about the impact of legislative reforms, community-led initiatives and the need for a commitment to Indigenous self-determination as defined by Indigenous people. It is crucial that these efforts are led by the voices and lived experiences of Indigenous women — not simply informed by those voices and experiences. Supported by Indigenous researchers and service providers in the space, we must prioritise culturally responsive, trauma-informed practices and a holistic approach to healing that addresses the interconnected needs of individuals, families and communities.

I am constantly reminded of the words of Mrs Sekai Holland, whose concept of the infrastructure of violence is so central to this work. There is life after violence. By working together, with Indigenous women at the forefront, we can dismantle the infrastructure of violence, challenge the systems that perpetuate it and create a future where all Indigenous women and girls are safe, respected, valued and empowered to thrive.

This is not just a task for some — it is our shared responsibility. This is not just a hope; it is our defiant resistance.

REFERENCES

ABS (Australian Bureau of Statistics) 2007, *Prisoners in Australia* (Cat no 4517.0), ABS.

ABS (Australian Bureau of Statistics) 2012, *Prisoners in Australia* (Cat no 4517.0), ABS.

ABS (Australian Bureau of Statistics) 2016, *National Aboriginal and Torres Strait Islander social survey, 2014–2015* (Cat no 4714.0), ABS.

ABS (Australian Bureau of Statistics) 2025, *Recorded crime—Offenders, 2023–24*, (Cat no 4519.0), ABS.

Aedy, R (presenter) 2018 (25 June), 'Sekai Holland: recovery from torture', *Late Night Live*, ABC Radio National, Sydney.

AIATSIS (Australian Institute of Aboriginal and Torres Strait Islander Studies) nd, 'The Stolen Generations', accessed 13 January 2026, aiatsis.gov.au/explore/stolen-generations

AIHW (Australian Institute of Health and Welfare) 2025 (February 28), 'Sexual violence', 2025, AIHW, accessed 24 July 2025, www.aihw.gov.au/family-domestic-and-sexual-violence/types-of-violence/sexual-violence

AIHW (Australian Institute of Health and Welfare) 2026 (February 24), 'Family, domestic and sexual violence: Aboriginal and Torres Strait Islander people, AIHW, accessed 30 March 2026, www.aihw.gov.au/family-domestic-and-sexual-violence/population-groups aboriginal-and-torres-strait-islander-people

Alexander, AJ, Nicholls, H and Plater, D (2023) 'The "incompetence" of Aboriginal witnesses in 19th century colonial Australia', in C Griffiths and ŁJ Korporowicz (eds), *English law, the legal profession, and colonialism: histories, parallels, and influences*, Routledge, pp. 139–173.

Alexander, M 2011, 'The new Jim Crow', *Ohio State Journal of Criminal Law* 9(1):7–26.

Allam, L 2022 (July 8), 'Alexander Berry: holes in the story of a NSW pioneer conceal past of Indigenous exploitation', *The Guardian*, accessed 26 June 2025, www.theguardian.com/australia-news/2022/jul/09/alexander-berry-holes-in-the-story-of-a-nsw-pioneer-conceal-a-dark-past-of-indigenous-exploitation

ALRC (Australian Law Reform Commission) 2017, *Pathways to justice: inquiry into the incarceration rate of Aboriginal and Torres Strait Islander peoples final report,* ALRC.

ALRC (Australian Law Reform Commission) and NSW Law Reform Commission 2010, *Family violence—A national legal response*, ALRC Report 114, Australian Law Reform Commission, ch. 25, paras 25.8–25.12, viewed 24 July 2025.

Alsalem, R 2022, *Violence against Indigenous women and girls: report of the Special Rapporteur on violence against women, its causes and consequences* (HRC/50/26), United Nations Commission on Human Rights.

Anderson, K 2016, *A recognition of being: reconstructing Native womanhood*, Canadian Scholars' Press.

Anderson, K, M Campbell & C Belcourt (eds) 2018, *Keetsahnak/Our missing and murdered Indigenous sisters*, University of Alberta Press.

Atkinson, J 1990, 'Violence in Aboriginal Australia: colonisation and gender', *Aboriginal and Islander Health Worker Journal* 14(2):5–21.

Atkinson, J 2002, *Trauma trails recreating song lines: the transgenerational effects of trauma in Indigenous Australia*, Spinifex Press.

Australian Government 2026, *Our Ways – Strong Ways – Our Voices: National Aboriginal and Torres Strait Islander Plan to End Family, Domestic and Sexual Violence 2026–2036*, Department of Social Services.

Baldry, E, B Carlton & C Cunneen 2015, 'Abolitionism and the paradox of penal reform in Australia: Indigenous women, colonial patriarchy, and co-option', *Social Justice*, 41(3):168–89.

Baldry, E & C Cunneen 2014, 'Imprisoned Indigenous women and the shadow of colonial patriarchy', *Australian and New Zealand Journal of Criminology* 47(2):276–98.

Bandura, A 2006, 'Toward a psychology of human agency', *Perspectives on Psychological Science* 1(2):164–80.

Barnett, OW, CL Miller-Perrin & RD Perrin 2010, *Family violence across the lifespan: an introduction*, Sage.

Behrendt, L 1993, 'Aboriginal women and the white lies of the feminist movement: implications for Aboriginal women in rights discourse', *Australian Feminist Law Journal* 1(1):27–44.

Bell, D & TN Nelson 1989, 'Speaking about rape is everyone's business', *Women's Studies International Forum* 12(4):403–14.

Berzeg, J & M Coello 2013, 'The quest for peace: Sekai Holland speaks to Janset Berzeg and Mariano Coello', *Refugee Transitions*, 27:39–41.

Bessarab, D & B Ng'andu 2010, 'Yarning about yarning as a legitimate method in Indigenous research', *International Journal of Critical Indigenous Studies* 3(1):37–50.

Blayden, L 2013, *Crimes Amendment (Zoe's Law) Bill 2013 (No. 2)*, e-brief no. 08/2013, NSW Parliamentary Research Service, NSW Parliament, accessed 24 July 2025, www.parliament.nsw.gov.au/researchpapers/Pages/crimes-amendment-zoes-law-bill-2013.aspx.

Bohn, DK 2003, 'Lifetime physical and sexual abuse, substance abuse, depression, and suicide attempts among Native American women', *Issues in Mental Health Nursing* 24(3):333–52.

Bottoms, T 2013, *Conspiracy of Silence: Queensland's frontier killing-times*, Allen and Unwin.

Bowden, A 1922 (20 May), 'Vanishing Aboriginals' [letter], *The Sydney Morning Herald*, accessed 24 July 2025, nla.gov.au, p 14.

Yellow Horse Brave Heart, M 1999, 'Gender differences in the historical trauma response among the Lakota', *Journal of Health & Social Policy* 10(4):1–21.

Bricknell, S & H Miles 2024, 'Homicide of Aboriginal and Torres Strait Islander women', *Statistical Bulletin* 46, Australian Institute of Criminology.

Broca, PP 1867, 'Broca on anthropology', *Anthropological Review* 5(17):193–204.

Bronfenbrenner, U 1994, 'Ecological models of human development', *International Encyclopedia of Education* 3(2):37–43.

Broome R 2015, *Fighting hard: the Victorian Aborigines Advancement League*, Aboriginal Studies Press.

Bunda, T 2020, 'The sovereign Aboriginal woman' in A Moreton-Robinson (ed), *Sovereign subjects: Indigenous sovereignty matters*, Allen & Unwin, pp 75–85.

Burbank, VK 1994, *Fighting women: anger and aggression in Aboriginal Australia*, University of California Press.

Burnette, CE & C Cannon 2014, '"It will always continue unless we can change something": consequences of intimate partner violence for Indigenous women, children, and families', *European Journal of Psychotraumatology* 5(1), doi.org/10.3402/ejpt.v5.24585

Carlson, B & T Farrelly T 2023, *Monumental disruptions: Aboriginal people and colonial commemorations in so-called Australia*, Aboriginal Studies Press.

Carlson, B, M Day & T Farrelly 2021, *What works? Exploring the literature on Aboriginal and Torres Strait Islander healing programs that respond to family violence*, ANROWS (Australia's National Research Organisation for Women's Safety).

Carlson, B, M Day & T Farrelly 2024, *What works? A qualitative exploration of Aboriginal and Torres Strait Islander healing programs that respond to family violence*, ANROWS (Australia's National Research Organisation for Women's Safety).

Cato, N 1993 [1976], *Mister Maloga: Daniel Matthews and his mission, Murray River, 1864–1902*, University of Queensland Press.

Cavadini, A 1972, *Ningla A-Na: hungry for our land* [documentary], Australian Film Institute.

Chauvel, C 1955, *Jedda* [motion picture], Charles Chauvel Productions Ltd, Australia.

Christie, N 1986, 'The ideal victim' in EA Fattah (ed), *From crime policy to victim policy*, Palgrave Macmillan, pp 17–30.

Collins, PH 1993, 'Black feminist thought in the matrix of domination' in CC Lemert (ed), *Social theory: the multicultural and classic* readings, Westview Press, pp 615–25.

Collins, PH 2002, *Black feminist thought: knowledge, consciousness, and the politics of empowerment*, Routledge.

Conor, L 2016, *Skin deep: settler impressions of Aboriginal women*, Apollo Books.

Coroner's Court of Western Australia 2016, 'Inquest into the death of Ms Dhu', findings delivered at Perth by State Coroner Fogliani, accessed 24 July 2025: www.coronerscourt.wa.gov.au/i/inquest_into_the_death_of_ms_dhu.aspx

Crenshaw, K 1989, 'Demarginalizing the intersection of race and sex: a Black feminist critique of antidiscrimination doctrine, feminist theory and antiracist politics', *University of Chicago Legal Forum* 1989(1):139–68.

Crenshaw, K 1991, 'Mapping the margins: intersectionality, identity politics, and violence against women of color', *Stanford Law Review* 43(6):1241–99.

Crenshaw, K 2016, *The urgency of intersectionality*, TEDWomen, YouTube video, accessed 24 June 2025, www.youtube.com/watch?v=akOe5-UsQ2o

Cripps, K 2011, 'Speaking up to the silences: Victorian Koori Courts and the complexities of Indigenous family violence', *Indigenous Law Bulletin* 7(26):31–4.

Cripps, K 2022, 'Could the Senate inquiry into missing and murdered Indigenous women and children prevent future deaths?', *The Conversation*, accessed 24 June 2025, theconversation.com/could-the-senate-inquiry-into-missing-and-murdered-indigenous-women-and-children-prevent-future-deaths-192020

Cripps, K 2023, 'Indigenous women and intimate partner homicide in Australia: confronting the impunity of policing failures', *Current Issues in Criminal Justice* 35(3):293–311.

Cullen, P, T Mackean, M Longbottom, J Coombes, K Bennett-Brook, K Clapham, R Ivers, N Walker & M Hackett 2022, *The First Response project: trauma and culturally informed approaches to primary health care for women who experience violence*, Lowitja Institute.

Cullen, P, T Mackean, N Walker, J Coombes, K Bennett-Brook, K Clapham et al. 2022, 'Integrating trauma and violence informed care in primary health care settings for First Nations women experiencing violence: a systematic review', *Trauma, Violence, & Abuse* 23(4):1204–19.

Cunneen, C 2001, *Conflict, politics and crime: Aboriginal communities and the police*, Allen & Unwin.

Daily Telegraph (Sydney) 1936 (3August), 'Criminal libel charge: Lubra's allegations', p 5.

Day, M 2020, 'Indigenist origins: institutionalizing Indigenous queer and trans studies in Australia', *Transgender Studies Quarterly* 7(3):367–73.

Day, M, B Carlson, D Bonson & T Farrelly 2023, *Aboriginal and Torres Strait Islander LGBTQIASB+ people and mental health and wellbeing* (Cat no IMH15), Australian Institute of Health & Welfare, Australian Government.

Deci, EL & RM Ryan 2012, 'Self-determination theory' in PAM Van Lange, AW Kruglanski & ET Higgins (eds), *Handbook of theories of social psychology*, Sage, pp 416–36.

Deer, S 2015, *The beginning and end of rape*, University of Minnesota Press.

Deer, S, B Clairmont, CA Martell & MLW Eagle 2007, *Sharing our stories of survival: Native women surviving violence*, Rowman Altamira.

DeGruy, J 2005, *Post traumatic slave syndrome: America's legacy of enduring injury and healing*, Joy DeGruy Publications.

Delgado, R & J Stefancic 2017, *Critical race theory: an introduction*, NYU Press.

Deslandes, A, M Longbottom, C McKinnon & A Porter 2022, 'White feminism and carceral industries: strange bedfellows or partners in crime and criminology?', *Decolonization of Criminology and Justice* (4)2:5–34, doi.org/10.24135/dcj.v4i2.39

Douglas, H, H McGlade, S Tarrant & J Tolmie 2020, 'Facts seen and unseen: improving justice responses by using a social entrapment lens for cases involving abused women (as offenders or victims)', *Current Issues in Criminal Justice* 32(4), doi.org/10.1080/10345329.2020.1829779

Du Bois, WEB 2019, *The souls of black folk: the unabridged classic*, Clydesdale.

Duran, E, B Duran, MYH Brave Heart & S Yellow Horse-Davis 1998, 'Healing the American Indian soul wound' in Y Daniele (ed), *International handbook of multigenerational legacies of trauma*, Springer, pp 341–54.

Dwyer, P & A Nettelbeck 2018, 'Savage wars of peace: violence, colonialism and empire in the modern world' in P Dwyer & A Nettelbeck (eds), *Violence, colonialism and empire in the modern world*, Palgrave Macmillan, pp 1–22.

Eades, D 2014, 'The politics of misunderstanding in the legal system' in J House, G Kasper & S Ross (eds), *Misunderstanding in social life*, Routledge, pp 207–34.

Farrell, H & V O'Sullivan 2025, 'Homicide, punishment and deterrence in Australia', *Southern Economic Journal* 91(4):1203–1235

Farley, M 2004, '"Bad for the body, bad for the heart": prostitution harms women even if legalized or decriminalized', *Violence Against Women* 10(10):1087–125.

Farmer, P 2004, 'An anthropology of structural violence', *Current Anthropology* 45(3):305–25.

Forbes, JD 2011, *Columbus and other cannibals: the Wetiko disease of exploitation, imperialism, and terrorism*, Seven Stories Press.

Foucault, M 1979, *Discipline and punish: the birth of the prison,* translated by A Sheridan, Vintage.

Foucault, M 1994, *Power: essential works of Foucault 1954–1984*, Penguin.

Fredericks, B 2008, 'Researching with Aboriginal women as an Aboriginal woman researcher', *Australian Feminist Studies* 23(55):113–29.

Fredericks, B 2010, 'Reempowering ourselves: Australian Aboriginal women', *Signs: Journal of Women in Culture and Society* 35(3):546–50.

Galtung, J 1969, 'Violence, peace, and peace research', *Journal of Peace Research* 6(3):167–91.

Galtung, J 1990, 'Cultural violence', *Journal of Peace Research* 27(3):291–305.

Galtung, J 1998, *After violence: 3R, reconstruction, reconciliation, resolution: coping with visible and invisible effects of war and violence*, Trancend.

Goldberg, DT 1993, 'Modernity, race, and morality', *Cultural Critique* 24:193–227.

Goodall, H 2008, *Invasion to embassy: land in Aboriginal politics in New South Wales, 1770–1972*, Sydney University Press.

Gray, S 1998, 'Black skeletons in a white man's cupboard: white men, Aboriginal women and the Stolen Generation' [Account of the 1936 criminal libel trial of a white newspaper editor, Charles Priest, resulting from his report of an Aboriginal woman's allegation of rape by a white police officer], *Overland* 150:79–82.

Griffin, R 2012, 'I AM an angry Black woman: Black feminist autoethnography, voice and resistance', *Women's Studies in Communication* 35:138–57.

Hargreaves, A 2009, 'Compelling disclosures: colonial violence and the narrative imperative in feminist anti-violence discourse and Indigenous women's writing', *Canadian Woman Studies* 27(2/3):107–13.

Harris, CI 1993, 'Whiteness as property', *Harvard Law Review* 106:1707–91.

Haskins, V 2004, '"A better chance"?—sexual abuse and the apprenticeship of Aboriginal girls under the NSW Aborigines Protection Board', *Aboriginal History* 28:33–58.

Haskins, V & J Maynard 2005, 'Sex, race and power: Aboriginal men and white women in Australian history', *Historical Studies* 36(126):191–216.

Heise, LL 1998, 'Violence against women: an integrated, ecological framework', *Violence Against Women* 4(3):262–90.

Herbert, X 2012[1963], *Disturbing element*, Allen & Unwin, Kindle edition.

Hiatt, LR 1996, *Arguments about Aborigines: Australia and the evolution of social anthropology*, Cambridge University Press.

Holland, S [T Smith] 2018, 'Dangerous times: Perspectives on torture, shifting global politics and respect for human rights', panel discussion, viewed 25 June 2025, www.youtube.com/watch?v=gTRWjN5OKlc 44:06–44:31.

hooks, b 1982, *Ain't I a woman? Black women and feminism*, South End Press.

hooks, b 1989, *Talking back: thinking feminist, thinking black*, South End Press.

hooks, b 2014, *Yearning: race, gender, and cultural politics*, Taylor & Francis.

hooks, b 2015. *Feminist theory: from margin to center*, Routledge.

Hoopes, MJ, J Dankovchik, T Weiser, T Cheng, K Bigback, ES Knaster et al. 2015, 'Uncovering a missing demographic in trauma registries: epidemiology of trauma among American Indians and Alaska Natives in Washington State', *Injury Prevention* 21(5):335–43.

Huggins, J 1987, '"Firing on in the mind": Aboriginal women domestic servants in the inter-war years', *Hecate* 13(2):5.

Huggins, J 1995, 'White aprons, black hands: Aboriginal women domestic servants in Queensland', *Labour History* 69:188–95.

Hunter, E 1993, *Aboriginal health and history: power and prejudice in remote Australia*, Cambridge University Press.

Ingram, S 2016, 'Silent drivers | driving silence: Aboriginal women's voices on domestic violence', *Social Alternatives* 35(1):6.

Innes, RA & K Anderson 2015, *Indigenous men and masculinities: legacies, identities, regeneration*, University of Manitoba Press.

Johnson, A 2016, 'Keep it coochie: reimagining the boundaries of race, gender, and sexuality in dominant hip-hop culture through raunch aesthetics', *The McNair Scholars Journal at Sacramento State* 17 (Cohort 2015–2016), 2017 National Conference of Black Political Scientists (NCOBPS) Annual Meeting.

Johnson, MP 2008, *A typology of domestic violence: intimate terrorism, violent resistance, and situational couple violence*, Northeastern University Press.

Kaberry, P 2004, *Aboriginal woman: sacred and profane*, Routledge.

Kipling, R 1899, 'The White Man's Burden', first published in *McClure's Magazine*, 12(2):290–291.

Kirzner, RS & M Miserandino 2023, 'Self-determination theory and social work values', *Research on Social Work Practice* 33(6):656–65.

Kortepeter, M (ed) 2001, *USAMRIID medical management of biological casualties handbook*, US Army Medical Research Institute.

Ladson-Billings, G & WF Tate 1995, 'Toward a critical race theory of education', *Teachers College Record* 97(1):47.

Langton, M 1988, 'Medicine square' in ID Keen (ed), *Being black: Aboriginal cultures in 'settled' Australia*, Aboriginal Studies Press, pp 201–26.

Langton, M 2018, 'For her, we must', *Griffith Review* 60:328–38.

Lattas, A 1992, 'Primitivism, nationalism and individualism in Australian popular culture', *Journal of Australian Studies* 16(35):45–58.

Liberman, K 1981, 'Understanding Aborigines in Australian courts of law', *Human Organization* 40(3):247–55.

Linklater, R 2014, *Decolonizing trauma work: Indigenous stories and strategies*, Fernwood Publishing.

Longbottom, M 2018 (June 8), 'Systemic responses continue to fail and traumatise Aboriginal women who survive violence', *IndigenousX*, accessed 25 June 2025, indigenousx.com.au/marlene-longbottom-systemic-responses-continue-to-fail-and-traumatise-aboriginal-women-who-survive-violence/

Longbottom, M 2020 (December 2), 'What will it take to acknowledge and respect our humanity?', *IndigenousX*, accessed 25 June 2025, indigenousx.com.au/what-will-it-take-to-acknowledge-and-respect-our-humanity/

Longbottom, M, Y Roe & B Fredericks 2016, 'Who is talking for us? The silencing of the Aboriginal woman's voice about violence' in SM Finlay, M Williams, M McInerney, M Sweet & M Ward (eds), *#JustJustice: Tackling the over-incarceration of Aboriginal and Torres Strait Islander peoples* (2nd edn), Croakey Health Media, pp 139–42.

Loomba, A 2015, *Colonialism/Postcolonialism*, Taylor & Francis.

Lorde, A 2007, *Sister outsider: essays and speeches*, Crossing Press.

Lowitja Institute, George Institute & University of New South Wales 2019, *The First Response project: trauma and culturally informed approached to primary health care for women who experience violence*, Lowitja Institute.

Luhrmann, B 2008, *Australia* [motion picture], Bazmark Films, Dune Entertainment III, Ingenious Media and ScreenWest, Australia, United Kingdom and United States.

Lui-Chivizhe, L 2022, *Masked histories: turtle shell masks and Torres Strait islander people,* Melbourne University Publishing.

Macdonald, G 2010, 'Colonizing processes, the reach of the state and ontological violence: historicizing Aboriginal Australian experience', *Anthropologica* 52(1):49–66.

Mayor, A 1995, 'The Nessus shirt in the New World: smallpox blankets in history and legend', *Journal of American Folklore*, 108(57):54–77.

McGlade, H 2012, *Our greatest challenge: Aboriginal children and human rights*, Aboriginal Studies Press.

McGrath, A 1984, *'Black velvet': Aboriginal women and their relations with white men in the Northern Territory, 1910–40*, Fontana Collins.

McGrath, A 1990, 'The white man's looking glass: Aboriginal–colonial gender relations at Port Jackson', *Australian Historical Studies* 24(95):189–206.

McGrath, A 2015, *Illicit love: interracial sex and marriage in the United States and Australia,* University of Nebraska Press.

Matsuda, MJ 2018, *Words that wound: critical race theory, assaultive speech, and the first amendment*, Taylor & Francis.

Maynard, J 2007, *Fight for liberty and freedom: the origins of Australian Aboriginal activism*, Aboriginal Studies Press.

Memmi, A 1965, *The colonizer and the colonized*, translated by H Greenfield, Beacon Press

Mercer, J 1975, *The other half: women in Australian society*, Penguin.

Meston, A 1896, *Report on the Aboriginals of Queensland*, Edmund Gregory, Government Printer.

Mills, C 2003, 'White supremacy' in TL Lott & JP Pittman (eds), *A companion to African American philosophy*, John Wiley & Sons, pp 269–81.

Moreton-Robinson, A 2000, *Talkin' up to the white woman: Aboriginal women and feminism*, University of Queensland Press.

Moreton-Robinson, A 2003, 'Tiddas talkin' up to the white woman: when Huggins et al. took on Bell' in M Grossman (ed), *Blacklines: contemporary critical writing by Indigenous Australians*, Melbourne University Press, pp 66–80.

Moreton-Robinson, A 2004, *Whitening race: essays in social and cultural criticism*, Aboriginal Studies Press.

Moreton-Robinson, A 2011, 'The white man's burden: patriarchal white epistemic violence and Aboriginal women's knowledges within the academy', *Australian Feminist Studies* 26(70):413–31.

Moreton-Robinson, A 2015, *The white possessive: property, power, and Indigenous sovereignty*, University of Minnesota Press.

Moreton-Robinson, A 2022, 'Monuments, place names and black lives matter: memorialising Captain James Cook', *Legalities* 2(1):67–81.

Moses, [A]D, *Genocide and settler society: frontier violence and stolen Indigenous children in Australian history*, Berghahn Books.

Mundine, W 2016 (October 3), 'Indigenous people must condemn family violence', *The Australian*, accessed 20 May 2025, theaustralian.com.au/opinion/indigenous-people-must-find-a-voice-to-condemn-domestic-violence/news-story/1670a3fe4f2651819f4625023b7c480f

Murphy, J 2013, 'Conditional inclusion: Aborigines and welfare rights in Australia, 1900–47', *Australian Historical Studies* 44(2):206–26.

Murphy-Oikonen, J Chambers, L McQueen, K Hiebert, A & Miller, A 2022, 'Sexual assault: Indigenous women's experiences of not being believed by the police', *Violence Against Women*, 28(5):1237–58

Nadal, KL 2018, 'A review of trauma literature and approaches' in KL Nadal, *Microaggressions and traumatic stress: theory, research, and clinical treatment*, American Psychological Association, pp 17–37.

Nakata, M 2007, *Disciplining the savages, savaging the disciplines*, Aboriginal Studies Press.

Nakata, M 2024 (July 24), 'Self-determining responses', paper presented at the Reframing the Conversation seminars, Indigenous Education and Research Centre, James Cook University.

Nakata, M & V Nakata 2022, *Supporting Indigenous students to succeed at university: a resource for the higher education sector*, Routledge.

Nakata, S 2015, *Childhood citizenship, governance and policy: the politics of becoming adult*, Routledge.

Nancarrow, H, K Thomas, V Ringland & T Modoni 2020, *Accurately identifying the 'person most in need of protection' in domestic and family violence law*, ANROWS (Australia's National Research Organisation for Women's Safety).

Nettelbeck, A 2013, '"Equals of the white man": prosecution of settlers for violence against Aboriginal subjects of the Crown, colonial Western Australia', *Law and History Review* 31(2):355–90.

NSW Department of Communities and Justice (DCJ) (29 March 2022) *New laws commence to better recognise loss of an unborn child due to criminal acts* [media release], accessed 24 July 2025: dcj.nsw.gov.au/news-and-media/media-releases-archive/2022/new-laws-commence-to-better-recgonise-loss-of-an-unborn-child-du.html.

New South Wales Government 1900, *Crimes Act 1900* (NSW). NSW Legislation.

Norman, H & AM Payne 2022, 'Nowhere else but home: a national resting place for Indigenous Australian ancestral remains', *Curator: The Museum Journal*, 65(4):817–834.

Nourse, V 1997, 'Passions progress: modern law reform and the provocation defense, *The Yale Law Journal* 106(5):1331–448.

NSW Domestic Violence Death Review Team 2017, *Report 2015–2017*, NSW Government.

Organ, MK 1990, *Illawarra and south coast Aborigines 1770–1850*, Aboriginal Education Unit, University of Wollongong.

Organ, MK 2014, *Secret service: Governor Macquarie's Aboriginal war of 1816*, University of Wollongong, accessed 20 May 2025, ro.uow.edu.au/articles/conference_contribution/Secret_Service_Governor_Macquarie_s_Aboriginal_War_of_1816/27845316

O'Shane, P 2002, 'Corroding the soul of the nation', *UNSW Law Journal* 25:212–15.

Panahi, R 2017 (August 30), 'Darebin council Australia Day ban divides Aussies', *The Herald Sun*, accessed 20 May 2025, www.heraldsun.com.au/blogs/rita-panahi/darebin-council-australia-day-ban-divides-aussies/news-story/43ca705458afc0efdaf81b4b8755180b

Parsons, K 2001, 'Structural violence and power', *Peace Review* 19(2):173–81.

Peternelj-Taylor, C 2014, 'Missing and murdered women', *Journal of Forensic Nursing* 10(4):185–6.

Queensland Government 2019 (11 April), 'About sexual abuse and assault', accessed 24 June 2025, www.qld.gov.au/community/getting-support-health-social-issue/support-victims-abuse/sexual-abuse-assault/about-sexual-abuse-assault

Rademaker, L & T Rowse 2020, *Indigenous self-determination in Australia: histories and historiography*, ANU Press.

Reynolds, H 1972, 'Violence, the Aboriginals and the Australian historian', *Meanjin* 31(4):471–77.

Reynolds, H 2004, *Fate of a free people*, Penguin.

Reynolds, H 2013, *Forgotten war*, NewSouth Publishing.

Robert, H 2001, 'Disciplining the female Aboriginal body: inter-racial sex and the pretence of separation', *Australian Feminist Studies* 16(34):69–81, doi.org/10.1080/08164640120038926

Roberts, D 2014, *Killing the black body: race, reproduction, and the meaning of liberty*, Knopf Doubleday.

Rodgers, D & B O'Neill 2012, 'Infrastructural violence: introduction to the special issue', *Ethnography* 13(4):401–12.

Saylors, K & N Daliparthy 2005, 'Native women, violence, substance abuse and HIV risk', *Journal of Psychoactive Drugs* 37(3):273–80.

Simpson, A 2014, *Mohawk interruptus: political life across the borders of settler states*, Duke University Press.

Simpson, A 2016, *Indigenous Feminisms Power Panel* (University of Saskatchewan), YouTube video, accessed 24 June 2025, www.youtube.com/watch?v=-HnEvaVXoto

Skinner, LE 1975, *Police of the pastoral frontier: Native police, 1849–1859*, University of Queensland Press.

Smallacombe, S 2004, 'Speaking positions on Indigenous violence', *Hecate* 30(1):47.

Smith, A 2015, *Conquest: sexual violence and American Indian genocide*, Duke University Press.

Smith, LT 1999, *Decolonizing methodologies: research and Indigenous peoples*, Zed Books.

Smith, Z 2020, '"The Great Australian Silence": sexual violence in Australian history', *History Matters* (University of Sheffield), accessed 24 July 2025, historymatters.sites.sheffield.ac.uk/blog-archive/2020/the-great-australian-silence-sexual-violence-in-australian-history

Smithers, GD 2017, *Science, sexuality, and race in the United States and Australia, 1780–1940*, University of Nebraska Press.

Solorzano, D, M Ceja & T Yosso 2000, 'Critical race theory, racial microaggressions, and campus racial climate: the experiences of African American college students', *Journal of Negro Education* 69(1/2):60–73.

Stark, E 2013, 'Coercive control' in N Lombard & L McMillan (eds), *Violence against women: current theory and practice in domestic abuse, sexual violence and exploitation*, Jessica Kingsley Publishers, pp 17–34.

Sullivan, CT & M Day 2019, 'Indigenous transmasculine Australians & sex work', *Emotion, Space and Society* 32:100591.

Sykes, RB 1975, *Black women in Australia — a history*, Penguin Harmondsworth.

TallBear, K 2019, 'Caretaking relations, not American dreaming', *Kalfou: A Journal of Comparative and Relational Ethnic Studies* 6(1):24–41.

Tatz, C 2016, 'Australia: the "good" genocide perpetrator?', *Health and History* 18(2):85–98.

Tehee, M & CW Esqueda 2008, 'American Indian and European American women's perceptions of domestic violence', *Journal of Family Violence* 23(1):25–35.

Tench, W 2009[1789], *Watkin Tench: 1788*, edited and introduced by T Flannery, Text Publishing.

The Horsham Times (Horsham, Vic) 1935 (5 February), 'Life story of Aboriginal woman', p 4.

The Morning Bulletin (Rockhampton, Qld) 1935 (23 February), 'Aboriginal woman's appeal', p 5.

The Zimbabwean 2015 (6 March), 'Dedicated to dismantling the infrastructure of violence' (interview with Sekai Holland), *The Zimbabwean*, accessed 24 June 2025, www.thezimbabwean.co/2015/06/dedicated-to-dismantling-the-infrastructure

Tolmie, J, R Smith, J Short, D Wilson & J Sach 2018, 'Social entrapment: a realistic understanding of the criminal offending of primary victims of intimate partner violence', *New Zealand Law Review* 2:181–217.

Tonkinson, M & V Burbank 2017, *Mortality, mourning and mortuary practices in Indigenous Australia*, Taylor & Francis.

Trask, H-K 1999, *From a native daughter: colonialism and sovereignty in Hawaii* (revised edn), University of Hawaii Press.

Truth (Sydney), 1936 (August 9), 'Gaoled for criminal libel: unusual case at Darwin', p 12.

Veracini, L 2010, *Settler colonialism: a theoretical overview*, Palgrave Macmillan.

Wacquant, L & G Steinmetz 2009, *Punishing the poor: the neoliberal government of social insecurity*, Duke University Press.

Walker, LE 1980, *The battered woman*, Harper & Row.

Walker, N, T Mackean, M Longbottom, J Coombes, K Bennett-Brook, K Clapham et al. 2021, 'Responses to the primary health care needs of Aboriginal and Torres Strait Islander women experiencing violence: a scoping review of policy and practice guidelines', *Health Promotion Journal of Australia* 32(S2):40–53.

Watson, PL 1998, *Frontier lands and pioneer legends: how pastoralists gained Karuwali land*, Allen & Unwin.

Wilkie, M 1997, *Bringing them home: report of the National Inquiry into the Separation of Aboriginal and Torres Strait Islander Children from Their Families*, Human Rights and Equal Opportunity Commission.

Williams, NM 1987, *Two laws: managing disputes in a contemporary Aboriginal community*, Australian Institute of Aboriginal Studies.

INDEX

ABOUT THE AUTHOR

Dr Marlene Longbottom is a proud Yuin woman, from the Wandi Wandian and Wodi Wodi clans from Roseby Park Mission (Jerrinja) on the south coast of New South Wales. Currently Associate Professor at the Indigenous Education & Research Centre at James Cook University, Marlene has been a dedicated advocate for Indigenous communities for more than 30 years, working as an Aboriginal Health Worker and in Indigenous policy and social justice across New South Wales and Queensland. Her practical experience grounds her academic work, ensuring that it remains deeply connected to the lived realities of the Indigenous communities she works alongside.

Defiant Resistance stands as powerful example of this commitment, drawing upon her decade-long research into the violence and harm experienced by Indigenous women and families. For the past 17 years, she has led community-based research and evaluation projects in urban, regional and remote areas of New South Wales and Queensland. Marlene's deep commitment to Indigenous agency and self-determination has been recognised through prestigious honours including a Discovery Australian Aboriginal and Torres Strait Islander Award (DAATSIA) from the Australian Research Council.

www.ingramcontent.com/pod-product-compliance
Lightning Source LLC
LaVergne TN
LVHW050955080826
845145LV00006B/1506

* 9 7 8 1 9 2 2 7 5 2 0 5 5 *